Trapped Life

Trapped Life

A Year with the Mandem on a London Estate

EBONY REID

#MERKY BOOKS

UK | USA | Canada | Ireland | Australia
India | New Zealand | South Africa

#Merky Books is part of the Penguin Random House group of companies whose addresses can be found at global.penguinrandomhouse.com

Penguin Random House UK,
One Embassy Gardens, 8 Viaduct Gardens, London SW11 7BW

penguin.co.uk

First published 2026

001

Copyright © Ebony Reid, 2026

The moral right of the author has been asserted

Penguin Random House values and supports copyright. Copyright fuels creativity, encourages diverse voices, promotes freedom of expression and supports a vibrant culture. Thank you for purchasing an authorised edition of this book and for respecting intellectual property laws by not reproducing, scanning or distributing any part of it by any means without permission. You are supporting authors and enabling Penguin Random House to continue to publish books for everyone. No part of this book may be used or reproduced in any manner for the purpose of training artificial intelligence technologies or systems. In accordance with Article 4(3) of the DSM Directive 2019/790, Penguin Random House expressly reserves this work from the text and data mining exception.

Set in 12.7/15.2pt Fournier MT Pro
Typeset by Six Red Marbles UK, Thetford, Norfolk

Printed and bound in Great Britain by Clays Ltd, Elcograf S.p.A.

The authorised representative in the EEA is Penguin Random House Ireland, Morrison Chambers, 32 Nassau Street, Dublin D02 YH68

A CIP catalogue record for this book is available from the British Library

ISBN: 978–1–529–91189–3 (hardback)

Penguin Random House is committed to a sustainable future
for our business, our readers and our planet. This book is made
from Forest Stewardship Council® certified paper.

In loving memory of Alvin Reid, who planted the seed of righteousness in my heart and inspired me to stand tall — strong in spirit and grounded in my roots. We miss you deeply, Daddy. If only you could see the tears still flowing from the family you left behind. This is for you, with all my love and gratitude. One love, always.

Contents

Introduction   ix

1. Cotch   1
2. Block   23
3. Shubs   49
4. Trap House   76
5. Mosque   113
6. Pen   137
7. Shebeen   168
8. Bookies   187
9. Church   204
   Epilogue   217

Acknowledgements   225
Notes   227

Author's Note

This story is based on an account of my experiences growing up in and around the London estate I call Northville, the pseudonym I have given the neighbourhood to protect the men I grew up with. It also incorporates some of the research I conducted over thirteen years ago with full respect for anonymity and confidentiality of those who feature in these pages. In crafting this story, I have intentionally merged some real-life people, changed the names of people and places, and in some instances have blurred the details of events to maintain privacy and anonymity. It is of course shaped by my own memory and interpretation. I have endeavoured to tell these experiences with care and respect.

Introduction

The year was 1997, and the summer holidays had just begun. I was in secondary school and was thrilled to put another school year behind me and start some fun adventures kicking around my estate. As a child growing up in an inner-city neighbourhood, summer meant the same thing it did for kids across the country: complete freedom. There were no alarm clocks, packed schedules or homework for at least six weeks. It was also a time filled with eager anticipation as I looked forward to reuniting with my friends Lorrie, Jacks, Neva and Cory at our usual hangout spot, the basketball cage. I had planned to meet everyone at noon, but I was running late. As I hurried to get dressed and fix my hair, the sound of my doorbell ringing startled me. I stumbled down the stairs, accidentally tripping over my cat, Ziggy, on the way. I looked up from the floor to see Lorrie's brown eyes peeking through my letterbox.

'Ebs, hurry up! We're going to be late!' she shouted, her voice rising above the sound of Maxwell's track 'Ascension' blaring in the background.

Every year, on 5 August, Lorrie's energy would skyrocket. It was the day of the annual basketball tournament, a fierce competition between Northville and a local team. Year on year, winning this intense match had become her ultimate obsession. We were all basketball enthusiasts, talking about the Chicago Bulls and the Los Angeles Lakers all the time, but Lorrie's love for the game was unmatched. She had aspirations of playing professionally and becoming the best female basketball player in history. Her height, athletic build and strength were clear indicators of her potential. Lorrie's ability to dunk like Michael Jordan and outshine even the most seasoned players in the community was a sight to see.

'Lorrie, are you mad? Why are you screaming through the door?' I burst into laughter, scrambling up off the cold marble floor. Despite landing on my hands and knees right next to Ziggy's food bowl, I couldn't bring myself to scold her. Lorrie's positive energy was like a contagion, spreading joy and laughter even in the most unexpected situations. It was a trait she'd had since our first day at nursery school, a quality that made her endearing. After wiping the muck from my cat's litter tray off my new Nike Air Max 93s, I quickly grabbed a slice of toast from the kitchen and stepped out into the sticky summer day. Lorrie was ahead of me, walking eagerly towards the cage when I closed my front door. I turned to follow her when someone unexpectedly grabbed my shoulder.

'What's up, Ebs? You good?'

It was Jacks. He was two years older than us, but we had bonded quickly. While other girls admired his good looks – his silky-soft cornrowed hair and bright smile – I was drawn to his soul. I loved his playful personality and how he always looked out for me.

As we navigated the rollercoaster of our teenage years, Jacks became my go-to source of calm whenever I felt self-doubt creep in. Our conversations were a fun mix of silly jokes and deeper discussions, almost as if we had our own secret language. Jacks just got me; he knew instinctively when I needed quiet or when I just wanted him nearby without any words. He listened so intently, making me feel as if every word I said mattered to him. In those moments, it was as though the rest of the world faded away, leaving just the two of us in our little bubble. What we had was special – different from my other friendships. It was a unique blend of trust and closeness, an inexplicable intimacy reminiscent of young love, even though we never dared to use the 'L' word or share a kiss. All I knew was that there was this strong invisible thread connecting us, an unspoken pact that we'd always have each other's backs, no matter what.

'Let's go fr-fr-front . . . l-l-line before we g-go cage,' Jacks stuttered, frantically scratching the eczema on his hands and ears. Back then, Jacks tended to get tongue-tied and pick at his skin whenever he felt anxious.

'Are you okay, Jacks?' I could smell the unmistakable odour of weed that drenched his white Champion T-shirt and overpowered his Issey Miyake cologne.

I leaned in for a hug and rested my head against his chest. 'It's b-been one of those days. Just follow me Frontline r-real quick nah.' Or, in other words, 'I need to find Frankie and get another draw, so I don't lose my shit.'

When Jacks didn't bun weed, he was depressed and impatient. Frankie, a well-known drug dealer and Jacks's cousin on his dad's side, was happy to accommodate his habit. Since they were family, Jacks got a discount and would buy a small draw of weed for £10 every day. Back then, he got high daily. This type of escapism was common among many kids coming of age in our neighbourhood of Northville. Like many impoverished council-managed public housing developments in the nineties, drugs weren't hard to come by. The drug trade was everywhere. Drugs and dealers were part of daily life; they were there, on every corner, deck and concrete stairway, peddling drugs twenty-four hours a day. Despite their prevalence, the Frontline was the epicentre. On a hot day like this one, you'd be sure to find Frankie there, as, like most street hustlers, he was a creature of habit.

The Frontline wasn't my favourite place to visit because of the people that usually hung out there, but going for walks with Jacks always felt like an adventure. He knew our neighbourhood like the back of his hand, effortlessly guiding us through the streets. With every turn, he would show me a hidden gem or a surprising spot in Northville, which I had never noticed before. Whenever we paused, he shared fascinating stories about the history of the area and the old Gs he admired. His words brought ordinary spots to life, creating vivid pictures of life in our community. Jacks had a special way of seeing the world around him, and his ability to showcase the charm of Northville was a skill I would hold on to as I got older.

Our walk to the Frontline took us along Sasha Street, crossing a flat stretch of open grass sprinkled with big trees until we reached K Park. It blended effortlessly into its surroundings, looking perfectly at home, as if it had always belonged there. K Park wasn't large, you could walk across it in under a minute, but it had everything we needed: two old swings that squeaked when you played on them, a climbing frame that was missing some important parts, and a brown slide that could scorch your legs on a sunny day.

But what made the park special wasn't the equipment; it was the people. It was always lively, filled mostly with local single mothers keeping an eye on their toddlers while sharing the latest neighbourhood news. K Park had become the go-to spot for gossip. You couldn't walk through it without overhearing stories about whose man had left, who was dating whom or who had beef and why. Just spending ten minutes there, you'd leave knowing more than you probably should.

We paused for a moment to watch one of our favourite characters, Stacey-Ann, who lived next door to Jacks. We affectionately called her the 'cartwheel queen'. Stacey-Ann, in her late fifties, could be found every day outside K Park, practising her cartwheels in her nightdress as if no one was watching. As Jacks and I strolled by, we marvelled at her acrobatic performances, cheering her on, making her face light up joyfully as she tumbled down the hill again and again. I loved seeing her beautiful brown, almond-shaped eyes shine happily whenever we encouraged her. Yet, outside of these moments, when she roamed the estate aimlessly, her eyes looked sad and filled with pain.

After we passed K Park, we strolled down a gentle slope. It wasn't steep, but it was just the right length for kids to race down on their skateboards. A few of them were at the top, ready to go. Jacks and I watched as one kid sped past and narrowly avoided crashing into a tree, only to enthusiastically rush back up for another turn. At the bottom, we reached Silver Street, a long, winding road that seemed to go in circles, even though we knew where it led. Lining the street were identical houses, all sharing the same colour and design. Their driveways varied. Some had cars parked neatly, while others were cluttered with wheelie bins left out from the night before.

I could hear the old Gs before I saw them, the roar of Kawasaki Ninjas, Yamahas, and Suzukis slicing through the air as they zoomed up and down Silver Street as if it was their own private racetrack. The late nineties were all about the superbikes. They grabbed everyone's attention with their loud exhausts and vibrant colours shimmering in the sunlight. The smell of burning rubber filled our nostrils, and a group of stylishly dressed women stood nearby, their outfits looking beautiful next to the sleek superbikes. With playful smiles, they exchanged glances, each hoping to be the next 'hot gal' to ride on the back of those legendary bikes.

Jacks teased me, 'That'll b-be you next year – hot gal, Ebs!'

I laughed and jumped on his back, saying, 'Hell no!'

We carried on at pace, until we reached Vinnie's, our local corner shop. You couldn't miss it as it was right on the corner, with a bright yellow sign that had seen better days – half the letters were missing, and the metal shutters sometimes got stuck halfway up. The shop was about the size of a small bedroom, but stocked all kinds of items you might need, from canned foods and cereals to light bulbs, lottery scratch cards and a freezer full of ice lollies, burgers, fish fingers and frozen chips. More than just a shop, it was a place where people gathered, and Vinnie, the owner, knew everyone by name. Even waiting in line for your 10p packet of Space Raiders often turned into a friendly chat with neighbours.

Right outside Vinnie's, the Q Block and Z Block towered above us, their worn structures and broken windows telling stories of the lives that had once filled them. For several decades, these tower blocks had defined Northville's skyline, but, as urban regeneration efforts began, they were reduced to empty shells, reminding us of the past and the uncertainty of what changes lay ahead.

Urban regeneration in Northville was a significant part of a larger initiative to revitalize social housing across London.

The goal was to breathe new life into some of the city's most struggling inner-city areas and build infrastructure to address the complex social and economic challenges faced by communities that had suffered years of neglect.

For many of us, urban regeneration was a memorable moment from our childhoods. The council promised our parents that this ambitious project would transform the area into a vibrant community filled with modern, stylish homes. We were told that these changes would create job opportunities for locals, improve access to services, reduce crime and enhance the overall quality of life for everyone who called Northville home. It was a hopeful narrative, one that promised to usher us into a new era of prosperity for our community. At least, that's what we were told.

Beneath that hopeful facade lay a deep sense of unrest within the community. The impending demolition of our old estate sparked considerable concern, as many residents felt their roots were being pulled up. I still recall the lively discussions during town-hall meetings, where passionate voices filled with frustration urged the community to hold on to our shared history. As teenagers, we might not have fully understood the deeper implications of these changes, but we certainly felt the weight of what was being lost. Places like the basketball cage and K Park, which shaped our lives and held our memories, were slipping away. We found ourselves powerless to stop the transformation that was altering the landscape of Northville and reshaping what home meant to us.

As we walked past the demolition site, we saw Mr Ali, who hailed from Afghanistan, reciting verses from the Holy Quran. We were spoilt with a diverse mix of cultures and ethnicities in Northville, from Irish to West African, Vietnamese and Bangladeshi families, although to many in the elder community Northville was also dubbed 'the Little West Indies' because of its large Caribbean population. We embraced our cultural differences and loved together peacefully and as one in Northville. Every Friday evening, Mr Ali's wife would share her food with her neighbours, creating a sense of community. Mr Chung was often skanking – a distinctive dance from Jamaica associated with ska and reggae – while chanting 'Jah Rastafari', alongside Samson, the local Rastafarian, during the annual Northville street parties.

I held Jacks's hand tightly as we approached the point that would bring us to the Frontline. It took us about fifteen minutes to get there, especially with all the pauses we made along the way, but every time I reached this spot an uncomfortable feeling settled into my stomach. Even though the Frontline was just a short walk from Vinnie's, it felt as if we were stepping into an entirely new world. The atmosphere shifted so dramatically that it seemed like the ground itself was warning us not to cross an invisible line. Our trainers crunched broken crack pipes beneath our feet. Strung-out addicts slumped in phone boxes. Sex workers waved down regular customers. People looking to buy drugs arrived by car or on foot. These were stark reminders that we had entered a different kind of place – somewhere we really shouldn't be.

When we arrived, the strong smell of alcohol and urine hit me immediately. Groups of men, both young and old, were gathered in loose circles on the Frontline, a large concrete area, surrounded by a few run-down shops. They leaned against the walls covered in graffiti, each mark telling a story of life in the hood, a record of those locked up or passed away too soon. Some men sat on the rusted metal railings, carefully watching everything around them. Dealers mingled quietly, exchanging subtle nods with people they recognized, while a constant stream of pedestrians hurried by, trying to stay unnoticed. The whole place felt charged, as if it was holding its breath in anticipation of something that was always bound to happen.

Gritting my teeth, I hurried past, feeling their curious stares on me. In the distance, I saw two plainclothes officers tussling with Jacks's cousin Frankie. His pregnant girlfriend, Sharon, was screaming at them. Jacks and I watched wide-eyed as the police officers threw Frankie to the ground, pressing his face against the concrete and tying his bloodied hands in handcuffs behind his back.

As teenagers, we were witnessing things in our community that no child should ever have to see, and I wasn't naïve. I knew I was growing up in a troubled neighbourhood. I would leave for school and return to people still in the same spot. I would hear about the robberies and other criminal activities from people around me. However, some parts of Northville felt different, almost insulated from the chaos that plagued places like the Frontline, and I came to understand the complexities of people's lives as I grew older.

Police sirens blared as Frankie was taken away in the back of a police van. I felt an overwhelming urge to escape from here, and all thoughts of Jacks's once-desired draw faded away. My heart pounded as we ran towards the more familiar part of our neighbourhood, Jacks holding my hand, comforting me, relief washing over us as we left the shadow world behind. We zipped past the church, laughter and soft hymns drifting from it as people dressed in white gathered outside. The old garage flashed by, its usual row of abandoned cars a blur as we turned on to Jill Avenue. Jacks didn't even glance at his favourite spot, where the tall horse chestnut trees stood, their spiky green shells always crunching under our feet. We reached the basketball cage in record time, both of us breathless.

Outside the tall, fenced area that surrounded the cage, we saw the familiar sight of Neva and Cory arguing. Although they were cousins, they acted more like arch-enemies than relatives. Jacks and I avoided another of the cousins' daily clashes and went straight to Lorrie, who was warming up for the upcoming match. Sweat dripped from her forehead as she moved through stretches and lay-ups. With a loud thump, the basketball bounced off the backboard and swished through the hoop. The net had been torn down during a previous game when Lorrie attempted to dunk and brought the whole thing down as she landed hard on the concrete court.

The cage sat proudly at the centre of our estate and was buzzing with energy, just as expected. This was where our lives intersected, where people of all ages found solace amid the chaos and crime that pervaded the Frontline. Kids came to play and have fun, teenagers showcased their skills and older folks gathered to watch and share stories from their own days. To me, it was the heartbeat of our community, a special spot where worries could be set aside, even if only for a moment.

Cory and Neva's uncle Horris was blasting music through his mini sound system while some of his friends were drinking Courvoisier and bunning spliffs. I was practising shooting with Lorrie while winding Cory up about his greasy lips, which resembled those of the rapper LL Cool J, when out of nowhere Bailey, a slightly older teenager from our estate who we all respected, hurried over to us with a gun near his waist.

'Run, get inside now and don't come back out until I tell you to,' he shouted. His eyes were nervous and darting between the basketball cage and the tower blocks. I held my breath, and in a split second five shots pierced the air in the distance, each bang slicing through the silence. I dropped to the ground, instinct kicking in, as a cold wave of fear flooded through me. Lorrie's delayed reflexes caused her to freeze, so I pulled her down beside Jacks and me, not letting go of her hand.

We were all terrified. None of us had ever seen a gun before and, in that moment, I disconnected completely, seeing Bailey, the gun, the chaos and myself lying on the ground with my friends from outside my body. I snapped myself out of my daze and began running so fast down the hill towards my house, bumping my head with Cory on the way. As I frantically tried to put the keys in my front door, I heard another round of gunshots, this time echoing loudly across the highrise tower block flats nearby. I thought I heard Bailey shout for help, but my imagination was continuing to play tricks on me, as he stood composed in the centre of the basketball cage, loading his gun, needing no help whatsoever.

He stood still for a moment, surveying the tower blocks before taking off and disappearing behind the flats. As I stepped through the doorway, my parents were relaxing in the kitchen, but quickly noticed something was off. I launched into a frantic explanation of the nightmare I had just witnessed, and their concern grew as they listened.

That summer, unlike any I had experienced before, suddenly felt like a prison sentence since I was grounded from going to the basketball cage. Even Lorrie's, Neva's and

Cory's parents put a pause on their summer adventures. What used to be a carefree summer now felt more limiting.

This was my initiation to neighbourhood violence and the brewing tit-for-tat territorial feuds that would wreak havoc and bloodshed in our community. Bailey escaped the ambush from a rival estate that day, but the incident set the tone for the months and the years to come. That summer unfolded with several incidents of gun violence, and in the years that followed four men I knew all died violently. I couldn't name it at the time, but I recognized that a disturbing phenomenon had gripped my community by the throat: a plague of murders among young Black men. The young men I'd grown up with were dropping like flies, killed by other local boys or men, most of whom would eventually suffer the same fate.

From my earliest memories, violence has overshadowed Northville, shaping its reputation as a dangerous and notorious gang area in London, particularly in the eyes of the police and local media, who often labelled it a high crime zone, reinforcing its image as a community plagued by problems. Yet Northville's early history was not always defined by these grim associations.

In the past, Northville thrived as an affluent area featuring middle-class housing for merchants and professionals. The community remained largely rural until the mid-nineteenth century, when industrial development began to reshape its character. Since post-war regeneration, Northville has undergone deindustrialization, demographic shifts and gentrification, with most recent efforts focused on erasing the scars of its troubled past.

Today, the local council proudly claims that Northville has

emerged as a symbol of successful urban renewal. It's easy to see why this perception has arisen; the transformation is striking, with little public space reflecting its historical landscape. The towering high-rise blocks have been replaced by a completely new living environment, featuring modern architecture in various contemporary styles and increased green spaces. Only the street names hint at the past, whispering stories of a different era. The notorious Frontline no longer dominates the scene. Instead, local shops and businesses have flourished in its place. Even the tone and pace of the community have changed, mirroring a far more peaceful atmosphere than before. This is the updated Northville with fewer illegal links. Despite this so-called ambience, an unmistakable sense of 'place sameness' remains,[1] but it has a different face.

Controversy surrounds the council's promise of renewed public space among the long-term residents, who struggle to participate in the project's regenerative framework, which appears to be designed for newcomers rather than the people who have lived in Northville for years.[2] While there are busy shops and businesses, the jobs promised have not significantly benefited the original residents, raising questions about the council's claims of inclusivity and promoting growth.

According to statistics from Trust for London, the borough where Northville is located remains deprived as of 2024.[3] Crime statistics also paint a bleak picture, with violent crime remaining high. However, what those statistics don't show is the reason why this is the case. What they fail to express is anything at all of the lives of people behind the statistics, and, as I grew older, it was the voices of the people in my community more than the reported statistics that told a clearer picture. The voices of young and adult men in Northville reveal their ongoing struggles: they remain in crisis as they confront the tough realities of their daily lives. As I write this, gunmen open fire outside a house party on the estate, fatally wounding two young boys. Currently, the streets in Northville are like a ghost town; the young boys and men on my estate are in a heightened state of anxiety, restricting themselves to short trips to the shops or friends' houses because the threat of being the next target is very real.

This reality is devastating and extends beyond the boundaries of Northville. The pervasive issue of street violence has become deeply entrenched, affecting communities across the UK. Major cities such as London, Liverpool and even Glasgow have grappled with high rates of violence for centuries. Glasgow was once infamously dubbed Europe's 'murder capital', a grim title that reflects the city's troubled history with crime.

Violence among young people has not remained static; it has experienced alarming cycles of surges and declines. The early 2000s marked a particularly dark period as incidents of street violence escalated dramatically. A defining moment during this time was the tragic stabbing of Damilola Taylor in 2000, which shocked the nation and highlighted the growing crisis of youth violence. Three years later, the gun-related murders of two young women in Birmingham sent ripples of fear and outrage throughout communities, prompting criminologists[4] to assert that these incidents ignited a new era of media obsession with street violence, particularly that linked to gang activity.

The year 2017 witnessed a devastating turning point, recording the highest number of deaths among children and teenagers due to violence in nearly a decade. Home Office figures from that year reveal the heartbreaking statistic of thirty-five young lives cut short by knife-crime-related injuries across England and Wales.[5]

In the wake of the Covid-19 pandemic in 2020, the grim reality of knife crime has continued to rise, painting an even bleaker picture. Reports indicate that knife crime has risen each year since the pandemic began. According to data from the Office for National Statistics, there was a twenty-one per cent increase in knife crime incidents during the most recent recording period. Specifically, between July 2022 and June 2023, there were 13,503 incidents.[6]

The most recent figures released by the Office for National Statistics reveal a further escalation of knife-enabled crime in England and Wales, which increased by four per cent in the year ending March 2024. Police recorded an alarming total of 50,510 offences during this period.[7] Over the past decade, the increase in knife crime has been striking, with an overall rise of seventy-eight per cent across the country.[8] Compounding the urgency of the situation, a report commissioned by the Youth Endowment Fund Charitable Trust published in 2025 highlights a critical disparity within this epidemic: Black children are disproportionately at risk of being victims of violence compared to other ethnic groups.[9]

These figures reveal only the sharp tip of the iceberg. What the raw agony and destructive street violence does to communities is mostly invisible from the perspective of those affected. The consequences of this issue are only ever superficially discussed by experts, and real voices rarely make the headlines.

Witnessing society's slow awareness and response to this grim reality is disheartening. There seems to be a collective numbness, as if the tragedies, a constant undercurrent of loss, have been normalized. It is chilling to consider the long-standing history of young and adult men from the inner city whose lives are cut short on street corners, in alleys, in local parks, outside nightclubs and within the very estates they proudly call home. Their stories echo through the inner city, yet for many residents in safer, more affluent neighbourhoods, these issues are distant concerns, almost too far removed to fully understand.

It is striking how entire communities can coexist while living in such starkly different realities. In places like Northville and other deprived inner-city neighbourhoods in London, people navigate their daily lives with a chronic sense of danger and fear, always aware of the threat of violence. In contrast, just a stone's throw away, other neighbourhoods are thriving in a bubble of privilege and comfort, where residents seem to glide through life with an unsettling indifference. This juxtaposition can be quite jarring and almost surreal. At times, I have felt as if I am living within a news headline others read with curiosity over breakfast, casually skimming past the harsh reality of pain and suffering that shape our world.

Street violence cast a shadow over my childhood, with police sirens, hovering helicopters and crime scenes blocked off with tape becoming familiar sights. Witnessing the fragility of life in such raw and visceral ways undeniably shaped me and influenced the path I took into academia. This story of trying to understand Northville, its residents and the cycle of crime and violence in which they are embroiled began on that summer day in 1997, but it started to take shape when I entered academia. I carried those memories of the years of bloodshed with me and was eager to find some answers.

The experiences of growing up in Northville found a voice in my BSc (Hons) and later in my Master's dissertation, but it was during my PhD programme that I delved into a deeper exploration of my lived experiences. Writing turned out to be a powerful way for me to make sense of the world around me, and with the support of the mandem – many with whom I grew up or who were childhood friends or neighbours – I pieced together my thesis. I felt a strong obligation to create a space within the academic discourse for their stories, which are often overshadowed by stigma and misunderstanding from those who have not experienced similar circumstances. Each academic paper I have written since has been a tribute to the lives and struggles of those who grew up in Northville.

As a female criminologist from the hood, which is a rarity in the predominantly homogeneous field of academia, I feel privileged to bring a fresh perspective to the table. My focus on masculinity, a topic that is typically underexplored among female academics, offers a unique vantage point. The intricate dynamics of how the mandem care for me and how I care for them, along with the mutual respect between us, are a significant part of this story.

However, I must admit that navigating my dual identity can be quite a balancing act. I often feel as if I'm walking a tightrope between being an insider who understands my community and an outsider who analyses it academically. When I shift into my 'academic mode', the probing questions and observational techniques can create a momentary detachment from the authentic connections I have forged within my community. Although being affectionately dubbed 'Dr Reid' is a source of pride, it sometimes creates a subtle distance between me and the relationships I have built in Northville.

Research can unknowingly create invisible barriers, which can feel isolating. I often worry that my community sees me as an outsider, someone who doesn't fully grasp urban life or the roots that have shaped me. It's a paradox – my genuine desire to explore and write about the raw realities of a place I call home can unintentionally alienate me from the very people whose stories I wish to tell.

Being an outsider is not always an easy position to hold. There are moments when I feel like a tourist, watching the daily struggles unfold around me, caught between familiarity and a sense of distance. Although I recognize the privilege of this position, it also weighs heavily, especially when I confront the disparities in our lives. Yet clarity emerges when I tap into my insider identity, particularly in those moments when the mandem share their stories with me – stories that resonate deeply because I have witnessed their struggles first-hand, like the traumatic memory of Bailey's attempted murder. It's in the quiet hours spent writing this book, surrounded by the sound of police sirens and hushed whispers of potential retaliation circulating on the estate, that I feel grounded in my insiderness. These experiences – both my own and those shared by the mandem – serve as powerful reminders of the environment that shaped me. This reality, one that I cannot easily shake off, fuels my commitment to honour the narratives of the mandem, including those we've lost over the years.

I'm still figuring out how to navigate my dual identity, one that blends my deep connection to my community with the insatiable thirst for knowledge that fuels my academic pursuits. I take immense pride in belonging to a community that recognizes and celebrates me as one of their own. At the same time, I embrace the role of a curious academic, dedicated to uncovering the layered stories and complexities that surround me. This unique balance has helped me find my voice, allowing me to share the mandem's stories through both our perspectives, blending personal insights with analytical understanding in a heartfelt dance of meaning. As both an academic and a resident of Northville, I approach the topic with both lived experience and intellectual interest. I employ the lenses of both worlds to convey their voices on the page, letting the mandem define, in their own words, the reality in which they live – a reality they refer to as 'trap life'.

By listening to mandem more attentively, their stories about trap life began to confirm and expand my own visceral understanding. They provided me with the language that I didn't have as a teenager, and that the academy could not provide. Trap life stems from the popular word 'trapping', or a 'trap house', connected to the act of selling drugs. It is commonly used by young and adult men who are 'on road', a phrase linked to specific UK street culture. Trap life describes not just being 'on road' – actively engaged in the lifestyle – but the relentless experience of feeling stuck: broke, disillusioned and with an array of negative influences that hinder successful transitions into mainstream society. Although 'trap life' is not a term commonly used by news media, politicians, police or even academics discussing street violence, it is an important concept I want to define and bring into public consciousness by highlighting the struggles through which the mandem have lived and survived despite the odds being against them.

Through these conversations, I began to grasp the various factors that blight their life chances and opportunities, and why young boys, trapped on the estate, particularly under threat of violence, often lose direction and feel hopeless. Places like Northville can be a nightmare for the human spirit. To survive, some of the mandem seek money and respect through illegal activities to overcome their socioeconomic disadvantages and status in life.

To say the lives and choices of young men growing up in the inner-city are limited is an understatement; the dysfunction runs deep. The realities of a lack of a good and consistent education and of limited employment opportunities, combined with the emotions that plague them – a sense of hopelessness, fatalism, sorrow and trauma – shape a daily battle often hidden from view. This complex lived experience rarely makes it into the public's vocabulary when talking about street violence and the survival tactics the mandem use to cope with adversity.

I often compare trap life to a shimmering oasis in the desert, an enticing mirage that offers relief from the struggles of living on the margins. Many mandem are drawn to the roads, believing in the dream of success that it promises. However, the harsh reality is that true success is elusive, and often celebrated narratives of rising from rags to riches are quite rare. As the mandem chase more money, status and respect, the emotional toll can be devastating when they reach adulthood with nothing to show for themselves but an existential crisis.

Through my academic research and writing this book, it has become evident that trap life is deeply influenced by psychosocial trauma. This trauma stems from a mix of psychological and social factors, which include emotional experiences, wounds from both the past and present, as well as the broader social context, such as neighbourhood conditions, family dynamics and the various social pressures and challenges faced on road. All these factors together complicate the process of integrating into mainstream society.

At its core, trap life embodies a relentless struggle for psychosocial survival set against a backdrop of limited opportunities and oppressive environments, which further damage identities. I've written this book with the understanding that many mandem in urban environments carry significant traumas. It's a mainstay in my academic research, which merges the subjective experiences of those affected by street violence with the objective realities of poverty and psychosocial trauma, and affects how I take you through this story.

The exploration of street violence through a psychosocial lens is relatively uncommon in criminology, despite its potential to provide valuable insights. While a few psychosocial criminologists, notably Gadd and Jefferson,[10] have made significant contributions through case studies examining masculinities and violence in Northern English towns, this perspective remains underappreciated. They advocate for a deeper understanding of individual biography, as well as what they refer to as 'psychic life', alongside the broader social context, highlighting the intricate interplay between the two. However, many criminology experts often overlook this perspective, focusing instead on superficial aspects of street violence, such as criminality. This tendency neglects how socioeconomically marginalized men of colour interpret, react to and respond to their lived experiences. To enrich the discourse, it is essential to reframe the narrative, examining the deeper struggles and intricate realities that shape individual choices and identities.

In this story, set within the complex world of the mandem,

I will introduce you to a diverse group of characters, each wrestling with their own struggles and hopes.

Among them, Aron stands out – a well-known 'badman' whose name carries weight across Northville. Hardened by the roads and the reputation that follows him everywhere, his tough exterior makes most people tread carefully. But beneath that armour is a sensitive soul – a poet who quietly wrestles with his emotions through verse. There's a toughness and vulnerability in him, yet the roads keep his true self hidden.

By his side is Cassius, affectionately dubbed his 'Dawg for Life'. He brings humour to the group, always quick to buss jokes and lift the mood, even in the midst of tragedy. But the laughter is a mask, a way to hide the trauma he's been through and the pain he can't show. His struggles run deep – silent and heavy – and no one ever sees them.

Then there's Ash, another close friend of Aron. Quiet and unassuming, he moves through life caught in a relentless cycle of misfortune – always in the wrong place at the wrong time. He doesn't seek the violence of the roads, but somehow it always finds him, dragging him back into a life that keeps taking more than it gives.

Another key member of the group is Andy, who was hesitant at first, but soon found himself pulled into drug dealing by the lure of quick cash. The reality, though, has been far more complicated than he expected. Every choice he makes carries consequences, and he's been struggling with the weight of those decisions – while his family quietly bears the pain, living with the fear and heartbreak his actions have caused.

Slightly older than the rest, Anthony lives with the growing awareness that life on the roads can't last forever.

He wants out, or at least part of him does. But the pull of the roads, the money, the status, the sense of purpose, is hard to let go, especially in a wider world that doesn't offer the same immediate rewards.

Not far from Anthony's struggles, Jacks wrestles with regret over entering the trap, struggling to imagine a brighter future. Beneath this burden is a gentleness of which he hasn't let go – a quiet refusal to become as cold as the world around him – but the roads are relentless. The violence, the violations, the constant pressure – it's all wearing him down. And, no matter how hard he tries to hold on to who he really is, that gentle part of him is starting to slip away.

In contrast, Jacks's cousin Mohammed has found comfort in his faith. Stepping away from the chaos surrounding his friends, he's embarked on a personal journey of reflection and redemption. His path offers a glimmer of light, a quiet reminder that, even in the darkest corners, there's still room for change, and maybe even healing.

In writing about the lives of the mandem, seven Black men and other characters who make their way into these pages, it's important to note that this grouping does not constitute a gang. Gangs have been a polarizing topic in society for decades and are often sensationalized by the media. Phrases such as 'knife-wielding gangs', 'organized gangs' and 'county lines drug gangs' frequently dominate headlines.

For example, a 2020 BBC report drew attention to a shocking story about a 'man stabbed by a knife-wielding gang'[11], and in 2024 the *Telegraph* shared a troubling account of a 'knife-wielding gang attack in a taxi'[12]. The BBC has also reported on organized gangs targeting vulnerable individuals, including children, and in 2019 they also mentioned 'more than 4,000 Londoners identified in drug gangs'[13], making a connection between county lines and gang activity. Such media portrayals tend to incite public fear and concern.

These depictions contribute to what sociologist Stanley Cohen termed 'moral panic', where a specific group is portrayed as a threat to societal values, leading to the creation of 'folk devils'. Cohen originally addressed this phenomenon in the context of the mod and rocker subcultures in 1960s England.[14] Today, similar patterns are seen in the sensationalized media portrayals of 'knife-wielding gangs' and 'county lines', which perpetuate negative stereotypes about Black youth, casting them as modern-day folk devils.

Among the concerns about Black males in urban areas, UK drill music – which has its roots in the Chicago genre – has also become a point of contention. A range of critics including MPs, police officials, tabloid media and segments of the public, argue that its lyrics and imagery glorify violence and gang culture. Some have gone so far as describing the music as 'demonic' and drawing connections between its artists and fatal stabbings in London. This heightened climate of anxiety and fear has led to increased sensationalist media coverage and a swift response from the government, including a heavy-handed approach by the police. Authorities have taken steps to censor music videos deemed 'gang-related', as part of the Serious Violence Strategy introduced in 2018 by the Home Secretary Amber Rudd under Teresa May's Conservative government, and in some cases have even invoked the Terrorism Act 2000 – legislation intended to address terrorism – to investigate drill music artists and their content. Additionally, the police have issued Criminal Behaviour Orders, gang injunctions, and threatened suspended prison sentences against some artists. There has also been an increase in the use of stop-and-search tactics, and intensified scrutiny of drill music videos. Sharing drill content on YouTube and other platforms can incur serious consequences, such as being classified as a gang member by the Metropolitan Police and added to the Gangs Violence Matrix.

The controversial Gang Violence Matrix (GVM),[15] used primarily by the police to monitor young Black males, was scrapped in February 2024 after a decade of operation. It became a symbol of disproportionate and racially biased policing in urban Britain. Its creation signalled a nadir of interest in the long standing 'gang talk', a narrative that has long unfairly criminalized Black men and boys residing in urban areas.

While you'll go on to read about the violence that consumes so much of the mandem's lives, what's rarely seen is their ambition to create meaningful identities and make sense of their lives and their time on earth. Their perspectives go deeper and further than the space and attention society has ever given them before. They take me beyond the Frontline, and further into Northville than I have ever been – not just geographically, but into the everyday places and deeper experiences that reveal the full complexity of their lives. The chapters in this book offer a deep dive into the heart of the inner city, as the private emotions of the mandem unfold in settings that form the backdrop to their daily lives. Wherever we spoke, they shared unfiltered, first-hand testimonies, and the surroundings always seemed to bring an underlying emotion to the surface. Here the mandem felt at ease revealing these to me, illustrating that their motivations are about much more than violence and criminal activity.

Captured in these chapters are remorse, anxiety and fear, but also pride, connection, laughter and hope – emotions that are universally recognizable as, at some point in our lives, we have all felt trapped, lost, abandoned, angry or gripped by fear. Their voices also reveal how crisis and trauma can impact us profoundly. Even the most destructive individuals on road have a range of sides to their personalities, offering a lens through which we can examine the universal human experience of pain and suffering.

In the upcoming chapters, I invite you to explore the world of the mandem by recounting a year spent in their company between 2012 and 2013. The narratives do not just reflect memories and experiences from the past, but also highlight the ongoing realities faced by young men in Northville and similar urban areas across the UK today. Northville represents many inner-city neighbourhoods in London, where young men and even older ones too, often feel isolated and constrained by their circumstances. While other parts of the city thrive, the mandem struggle with feelings of being overlooked and trapped, rarely experiencing the freedom and opportunities that the wider metropolis has to offer.

As we journey through this story, I'll take you to different locations, charting my way through these places and unveiling the intricate narratives they hold. Each one tells its own story reflecting the complex lives of the mandem, where moments of friendship, love, joy and dreams intertwine with tales of conflict, violence and heartbreak. Through these experiences, the interconnected threads of their lives will gradually unfold, revealing the dualities of their existence and the resilience that defines them.

In Chapter One, I welcome you to into the cotch, a lively gathering place cherished by the mandem. More than just a location, it serves as a comforting sanctuary where friends gather to chill, unwind and disconnect from the realities of life outside.

In Chapter Two, we step on to the block, another gathering spot for the mandem. This lively location serves as the heartbeat of their social lives, where ambition and bravado intertwine. Here, it's all about 'stunting' and 'flossing' – looking good and making an impression on others. But beneath the laughter, pageantry, and good times lies an undercurrent of danger.

Chapter Three takes us from the estate to a shubs. While raving in London can be an enjoyable and carefree experience, nights out for the mandem carry significant risks, especially for those compelled to defend their masculinity.

Chapter Four invites you into a trap house, offering insight into the lives of a diverse group of trappers often overlooked in mainstream discussions about drug dealing. The remaining four chapters delve deeper into critical themes, such as the role of religion, the perspectives of the community elders and the long-term consequences of the lifestyle.

I hope these stories will be meaningful and contribute to the ongoing discussions on serious violence in the UK. Perhaps they will also spark a conversation about our collective responsibility to listen, learn and empathize with those struggling to overcome trauma. This is particularly important as we become more aware of the power of collective action and the terrifying levels of inequality in our society. I aim to offer a balanced perspective that acknowledges the challenges faced by those who grow up poor and excluded in a wealthy society. They yearn to belong and live a better life. I dedicate this book to all the mandem who are trapped on road, whose internal battles have been silenced for too long and who have been troubled by all the stories they still cannot tell.

CHAPTER 1

Cotch

Aron's mother, Leanne and I hang a birthday banner on her front door, grinning excitedly at each other. Today is a special day because it's her son's twenty-third birthday. On this breezy Saturday afternoon, her house, also known as the Cotch, is bustling with people hurrying to prepare for the surprise birthday party. Her front door is wide open, allowing the mix of Caribbean food and the unmistakable scent of marijuana to waft through the air. Leanne takes charge, directing her hired 'staff' (residents of Northville) with authority. The local DJ, Errol, contributes to the atmosphere by blasting vibrant reggae tunes from his car as he sets up the sound system in Leanne's living room. Dicky the jerk man manoeuvres his steel jerk pan from his sizable white van. Vinnie hauls in crates of assorted alcoholic beverages from his corner shop. Amidst the organized chaos, Aron's girlfriend, Shyanne, enters, struggling with a set of personalized number balloons. Aron's annual birthday celebrations are extraordinary as they bring the entire neighbourhood together in one place. It's common to encounter people you haven't seen in years, and the mandem fill the street.

The scene hums with frenzied but efficient activity. Even I'm racing around, trying to be in all places at once whilst bringing in my contribution of fried chicken. The night before, Leanne had warned everyone not to show up with their 'two long han', a common phrase in patois, meaning people shouldn't arrive somewhere empty handed, but with an offering of food and drink.

The Cotch is a familiar and popular meeting place for Aron's friends most evenings, especially on weekends. They come here to relax, play video games, and be together. The home his mother has built has always accepted them. Leanne is the heart of her home and, her community. In many inner-city communities, there's a mother figure like Leanne, someone who looks out for everyone around her. Generous and compassionate, Leanne goes above and beyond to help those in need, and she is well known for her kind heart. Her wild, frizzy curls are her trademark, perfectly framing her warm smile and expressive face. People admire her nurturing personality, which has earned her the respect of the community. Leanne has a special talent for making everyone feel seen and heard, and she knows how to lighten the mood during awkward moments with her gentle approach. But don't be fooled by her soft-hearted demeanour; she's also strong and assertive. Just like her son, she speaks her mind and will not hesitate to 'tell you about yourself' and reprimand you when necessary.

Leanne has been a resident of Northville for many years and has witnessed the area's regeneration. She knows the community well and has been a valued member for a long time. Aron affectionately calls her 'Northville' because she is familiar with everything that goes on in the area. She shares her home with her other son Zak, who is older than Aron. Since I've been coming to her house, it's undergone a significant transformation. Before, the living room had bright orange walls and an old cream sofa, which got dirty easily and showed every stain from all the many gatherings she had hosted. Recently, she gave it a makeover, opting for softer colours on the walls and a stylish leather sofa that adds elegance while inviting relaxation as you sink into the plush, cosy cushions. In the middle of the room, a glass coffee table is decorated with unique ornaments, each telling its own story. Two tall artificial palm trees in the corners add a nice touch to the decor. Above a shelf filled with her impressive record collection, a large flat-screen TV is mounted on the wall. Like many people in Northville, where renting is common, Leanne takes great pride in her home and has created a warm and welcoming living space full of her personal touches.

As I take in the elegant room, my eyes are drawn to a collection of childhood photographs meticulously arranged on the shelves and walls. Among the photos that capture family memories is a professional family portrait with Leanne and her sons. Aron's beaming grin stands out, reminding me of a Cheshire cat, and seeing it brings a wave of emotions that makes it hard to hold back my tears. Struggling to compose myself before others notice my distress, I feel Leanne's comforting embrace as she hugs me from behind.

'Don't cry. He's still with us. By the grace of God, he's made it through another year.'

'I just wish every day could be as joyful for him,' I murmur, dabbing at my tears with my sleeves.

Birthdays are usually happy occasions, but for Aron and his family they carry a deeper meaning. Each one is a chance for reflection, especially for his mother. It's a moment to remember how fragile life can be, particularly for Aron growing up in Northville. Despite the dangers he faces, Aron is still here, and that alone is reason to celebrate. Days like this are a reminder that his life – and the lives of all the mandem – could be cut short at any moment. We could just as easily be mourning a loss instead.

Aron has faced threats for as long as I've known him. In Northville, violence shapes you in ways that you do not always see coming. Just last week, two masked gunmen opened fire as Aron and his best friend, Cassius, walked home.

The doorbell rings, jolting me from my swirling thoughts. I rush to answer it and find Bella, Aron's cousin, standing in the doorway, looking startled. Her long, burgundy hair is tangled in her fingers, a sign of her agitation.

'Is he here?' she asks, taking a swig from a bottle of Moët champagne.

'No, he hasn't arrived yet,' I reply worriedly.

Leanne had planned for Bella to take Aron out for lunch as a pre-birthday treat, allowing her to prepare for the party scheduled for 7 p.m. This arrangement would keep Aron entertained and give Leanne the time she needed to decorate the house and gather friends and family. Unfortunately, the plan went awry when Bella called Leanne to report that Aron was acting suspiciously after they returned home around 4 p.m. He thought Bella was hiding something from him, and after that, she hasn't seen or heard from him.

The news sends Leanne into a state of immediate panic. She starts pacing the living room, her high heels clicking on the wooden floor as she nervously flicks ash from the cigarette into the nearby ashtray. Taking a deep breath, she turns to me, her wide eyes searching mine for reassurance.

'Do you think he'll like the surprise? I want to make today special for him.'

I mask my dishonesty with a forced smile, responding, 'Yes, he'll love it,' hoping she won't sense the insincerity in my words.

Aron dislikes surprises or grand gestures because they tend to make him anxious. I've always assumed this is due to the unpredictability and uncertainty in his life, and his desire to avoid being caught off guard. I feel guilty about lying to Leanne, but I cannot find the courage to confess. I know it will crush her. Leanne has put a lot of effort into planning the perfect birthday celebration for Aron, and I don't want to ruin it for her. She ordered a birthday cake in his favourite colours, hired Jamaican caterers and even arranged for a special appearance by Mayhem, a famous local rapper. She hasn't overlooked any detail, even replacing the chandelier with a dazzling disco ball that lights up the room with colourful reflections. Since she has invested so much love and attention in planning this special day, telling a little lie feels like the kindest thing to do, especially because the celebration is more about her than Aron. Deep down, Leanne knows that Aron doesn't really like all the attention that comes with birthdays, but they give her a chance to escape and distract herself from the challenges they both face, while also bringing family and friends together. Each year, her efforts grow as she tries to make the parties even more amazing than the last, ensuring that the day is memorable for both her and those who love Aron.

'I'm just so fed up,' Leanne sighs heavily. 'I asked Bella to do one simple thing, and she couldn't even get that right.'

Bella had been warned not to come to the house with Aron, but here she is without him, anxious and scared. She paces around, trying frantically to get in touch with Aron and sending urgent messages to anyone who might know where he is.

'I'll never live this down!' she shouts. She is visibly drunk, swaying from side to side, and ends up vomiting on the welcome mat outside. I stand beside her as she tries to compose herself. The last thing I want, or need, is a full-blown argument with her. I have seen the transformation of her temper when she drinks, and I wisely wish to keep myself out of the line of fire.

Bella understands Aron better than anyone else. She knows he doesn't like being caught off guard. However, she went against her instincts and broke their trust by being part of the plan to get him away from the estate. Aron is not one to forgive easily and values loyalty above all else. Once you cross him, there is no going back. Bella knows it will take a lot of time and effort to regain his trust and make things right. They had only recently broken their painful silence – a two-month period during which Aron had coldly ignored her after finding out she spoke to his girlfriend, Shyanne, while they were on a break. In this moment of desperation, she's frantic to find a way to reconnect with him, determined to avoid experiencing his silent treatment again.

'Please call him for me. Tell him I'm sorry. Please do that for me, man,' Bella pleads, cradled in the arms of her best friend, Mary.

'I don't want to get involved. It's between you and Aron,' I reply, trying to look busy so she won't ask me again.

Outside Leanne's house, I take in the lively atmosphere, filled with laughter, friendly conversations and a positive vibe as people gather to celebrate Aron's big day. There are already more than fifty guests, and it's still early. The street is busy with the cheerful voices; cars are parked everywhere, some even double parked along the kerb. Aron's neighbour, Sanchez, blasts music from his Audi, adding to the joyful mood. A group of young women, dressed to the nines, approach Leanne's house. Among them is Maria, who lives just a few doors down from Aron. She eagerly scans the crowd, anxiously waiting for him to arrive.

'I can't wait to see Aron. I hope he notices my outfit,' Maria says with enthusiasm to her friend.

'Don't get your hopes up. Shyanne will be here, and he won't even pay you no mind,' her friend responds. Shyanne and Aron have been together since they were teenagers. Now that they are both in their twenties, they were inseparable, but that didn't mean other women didn't try to get his attention.

Maria looks stunning in her black dress and designer high heels. All the women who have come out today are wearing extravagant outfits with thigh-high designer boots, matching sunglasses and handbags. They sport various colours of lace-front wigs that reach down to their thighs, flawless make-up and excessive jewellery. They remind me of the women in the 1997 movie *Dancehall Queen*[1] setting, the standard for fashion and style in the Black community. As I turn to go back into Leanne's house, I recognize a voice calling my name. It's Cassius, a familiar face and extended member of the family to Aron, Zak and Leanne. Despite only having two biological children, Leanne has taken on the role of a surrogate parent to many of Aron's close friends. She seems to relish being a protective and supportive figure to her extended flock, nurturing them, looking out for them and treating them as one of her own.

Cassius rarely spends time at his own place. He's been welcomed into Leanne's home and her family's lives as if he's always belonged. There are light-hearted moments when Aron jokes that Cassius gets more attention from Leanne than he does. One Christmas, she gave Cassius a gift – a onesie that read: 'Leanne's third son'. It was funny, but also telling; it showed just how close they have become over the years. Leanne still laughs when she tells the story of the time Cassius came crashing into her garden one morning, trying to outrun the police. Dressed in just his boxers and one sock, he landed straight in a patch of stinging nettles. The antihistamine he was given caused an allergic reaction, and he had to be rushed to the hospital, much to Leanne's concern at the time, and amusement ever since.

'I'm sorry I missed your call earlier,' Cassius says.

I had contacted him that morning to find out where Aron was.

He lights his spliff, and the conversation drifts towards whether he has any idea where Aron has been hiding. Just as he's about to tell me, his expression changes.

'There he is!' he shouts, suddenly animated.

We both hurry back into the house after spotting Aron approaching.

Inside, Leanne is busying herself tending to everyone else – she's plating up food for Aron's old school friends, Solomon and Howard. In the middle of this, she's also setting up the ironing board to press Aron's cousin Pedro's shirt as he has forgotten to do it himself. Cassius swiftly embraces Leanne and whispers, 'Aron is on his way.'

Without missing a beat, Leanne stumbles over the ironing board, rushing past us to turn off the lights just in time for Aron to enter the room, and everyone inside erupts into a loud 'surprise' and releases their party poppers.

Aron barely has time to take off his coat before Leanne hurries over and gently kisses his left cheek. It's a little past 8 p.m., and Aron is looking sharp. He's even cut his long cornrows and now sports a fresh trim that matches his sophisticated red velvet blazer, white polo neck, straight black Armani jeans and black suede Clarks boots. He's with his friend Fraser, who just got out of prison a week ago. In sharp contrast to Aron's polished look, Fraser wears a worn grey tracksuit, paired with battered white Air Force 1s that have clearly seen better days.

'Where have you been?' she asks softly.

'Just been at Geoffrey's getting a trim, Mum.' But Leanne quickly catches the scent of alcohol on him and cusses him. Aron attempts to calm her down, explaining that he has only had a couple of Magnums to take the edge off. I sense something is troubling him. He seems preoccupied. His eyes are sad, and he appears to be avoiding the living room, preferring to stay in the hallway. I make my way to him to wish him a happy birthday, but Fraser intercepts, taking hold of my arm, and enquiring shyly how I am. I can't help but notice a stark difference in his appearance from the last time I saw him, a few years before he went to prison. Fraser was popular with the ladies and known as a sweet boy. Now, at just thirty years old, he is prematurely balding and he carries the weariness of a man much older. Deep bags frame his dull, sunken eyes, and he has a blank stare, removed from any surface emotion. He avoids eye contact and seems disconnected from his surroundings and the people around him. I try to keep the conversation going, but he starts to ramble, speaking incoherently, and getting caught up in old memories.

'You know dem man wanna hurt man. Man was walking in

the endz. Some car pulled up – man had to bad man up. They couldn't step to man. You know Geoffrey – he begs it – but man is badder than him, cos man don't know. Man is a soldier; man will back it, innit. What you saying, though, you good, though. Man been away for time. Man is out now, though. Man has to get on this ting again. Man is deya, though.'

Fraser continues to speak, reminiscing about his life on road, repeating the word 'man' between each word as he speaks rapidly, making it difficult for me to keep up.

'Watch now that I'm out. I'm gonna make some proper P. Aron is gonna take man to the JDs to get some new kicks, then man is gonna hit the clubs, drink some Henny and find me two gals. The galdem love man, because man had P.'

The world has undoubtedly changed since he went to prison six years ago, at the age of twenty-four, yet Fraser's psyche is still trapped in that time.

His adolescent state of mind – recalling his notoriety when he was younger, the fame he enjoyed, and his desire to indulge in the nightlife that once exhilarated him – can be attributed to two factors: firstly, the extensive time he spent behind bars and, secondly, that he mentally emerged from prison the same age he went in. Psychologists refer to this as 'age regression',[2] and it's a coping mechanism where the person mentally retreats to a younger age to deal with stress, anxiety or trauma.

Fraser faced numerous challenges growing up, and his time in prison only exacerbated them. During the time I knew him, he had often been homeless, crashing on friends' couches due to strained relationships with his family. Fraser didn't share this information, but I learned from Cassius and some of the other mandem that he had been hospitalized multiple times for drug-induced psychosis.

Fraser's life was sadly typical of a young man looking for an escape from his harsh reality, temporarily finding solace in his addictions to drugs, clubs and women. He was also heavily immersed in the roads, robbing to gain wealth and status in Northville before his last prison sentence. He was caught up in a cycle of crisis and crime and would do anything not to feel his pain and unworthiness, and this gnawing sense of shame from living on the breadline kept him going back to prison. He'd been in and out of jail since he was fifteen years old. Since then, he'd had a mixture of long and short stints in prison. Fraser had lived more of his life in jail than on road.

Among the mandem, I heard various stories of Fraser's repeated imprisonment. Aron had always blamed Fraser's mother, saying she prioritized her romantic relationships over her own son. I also heard Cassius mention that Fraser had become institutionalized – preferring prison to the real world – and I can see why Cassius might think that. Standing next to Fraser, I notice his anxious demeanour and hypervigilant behaviour. He stands with his arms tightly crossed, his posture is defensive and each time the doorbell rings he is visibly startled.

As I'm about to ask him a question, Aron hurries over, seemingly picking up on my concern, and asks if Fraser is causing me any trouble. Aron gives me a hug, and it's our first chance to talk since the beginning of the party. When I assure him I'm fine talking to Fraser, he leans in closer and asks, 'Are you sure?' before turning to address his friend.

'Fraser, what's wrong with you, my G? Why are you standing like that? Are you a mad head? You know you ain't in the cell no more, right? Sort yourself out real quick.'

Although Aron's remarks are light-hearted, Fraser's vacant expression becomes increasingly worrisome, and he withdraws further into his thoughts, distancing himself from the party.

'My brudda, drop my bag in your room. Auntie Leanne said she's cool with me staying the night. I need to head out real quick.' Fraser looks past everyone and heads towards the door. Worried, I ask him to stay in the house.

'Allow it. Don't worry, man. He'll be good,' Aron says, reassuring me. He then turns to Fraser and tells him to come straight back, while giving him a fist bump.

Each time Fraser was released from prison and returned to Northville, he seemed to have lost a part of himself. To those around him, this was a familiar sight, but for me it was heartbreaking to see him become even more distant with each release. I always thought Fraser was the most vulnerable among his friends because he was struggling with mental-health issues he didn't know how to articulate, let alone deal with. Apart from Aron, no one else in the group was willing to acknowledge this. His struggles were often the subject of jokes among the group, many of whom were also fighting their own battles and trying to cope with poor mental health.

Openly discussing mental health is not a common practice within the Black community. Research by the Race Equality Foundation[3] shows that individuals from Black and minority ethnic communities experience poorer mental-health outcomes compared to other groups, yet they are less likely to seek support. Due to social stigma and cultural taboos, this topic is often avoided, discouraging individuals from asking for help. Many of us have heard a well-meaning elder in our family tell us to 'toughen up' and 'stay strong' when we express our worries, reinforcing the message that our feelings should be kept private, that sharing them is somehow a sign of weakness. They come from a different generation where they had to persevere rather than pause. Cultural and societal pressures often reinforce stereotypes about mental health struggles, labelling people as 'crazy' or a 'mad head', as Aron refers to Fraser. On top of this, dominant ideas of masculinity, especially within road and street culture, make it even harder for the mandem to express vulnerability. While some progress has been made in recent years with the emergence of Black men's support groups,[4] stigma, limited visibility and a culture that discourages emotional honesty often make these spaces feel out of reach for the mandem.

The atmosphere at Aron's party is buzzing with energy just after 10 p.m. as the crowd belts out the lyrics to Damien Marley's track 'Beautiful'. Laughter and chatter mix with the beats as everyone enjoys their drinks. Amid the lively scene, Aron, Cassius and Pedro gather around Leanne's wooden circular table, deeply engrossed in a game of cards. Leanne hurries into the kitchen as the lights begin to dim, on a mission to retrieve Aron's birthday cake. Suddenly, a loud car horn blares outside, followed by flashing lights. The noise startles us, and we rush outside to see what's happening. Fraser is on the ground, blood gushing from his right hand where he fell on his knife. A car speeds off into the distance before anyone can make out the registration number. Leanne rushes to him, and Aron and Cassius are right behind her. They help Fraser to his feet, but as soon as he stands he takes off, running. He ducks and weaves through the parked cars and partygoers, sprinting up and down the street, searching for the person who ran him over.

Fraser's cream jumper is stained with blood. He rips it off and shouts, 'Does this man know who I am? Man is a badman man! I will murder him.' He is furious, yelling so everyone on the street can hear. Eventually, he tells us it was someone he had beef with before going to prison. They crossed paths at Vinnie's, and Fraser managed to escape by headbutting him in the face. But he wasn't finished. He followed Fraser to Leanne's in his car, where the rest of the violence broke out. Fraser couldn't believe the man had the nerve to confront him again after all these years.

He spots Aron and Cassius in the crowd and tells them who he is. 'Man is a badman. Man will fuck a man up. Man is trying to take man for a pussy.' He paces, eyes sharp, urging them to 'ride out' – to team up with friends and back each other during conflict.

Before Fraser was institutionalized, he craved respect from everyone in Northville. He was known as a disciplinarian, a man with standards, willing to go to war over even the smallest disputes. He didn't bend. He didn't forgive. And he didn't forget a grudge. Now, Fraser is fighting hard not to be seen as vulnerable. He's refusing to show any strain under pressure. He wants to look tough – anything but weak. On his third lap round the block, Leanne finally reaches out, grabbing his hand, pulling him close. She holds him tight, pleading with him to come inside and not ruin Aron's birthday. She gently presses a tea towel against his hand to stem the bleeding and strokes his face to calm him down. Her words and touch instantly soothe the turmoil inside, bringing him back to the present moment. I see his face soften, and his body language shifts. Under his breath, he murmurs his apologies for bringing chaos to her door and to Aron's birthday. These are the most coherent words he's spoken all night. Defeated yet at peace in Leanne's arms, he is safe now. He is home.

When Fraser was released from prison, he was unsupported by his family, had no money and was battling undiagnosed mental-health issues, which were worsened by the violence he experienced on road. Like many of Aron's friends, Fraser, would go straight to Leanne's house after being released or in times of need. Her home conveys a strong message of safety, acceptance, love and, most importantly, family. In these moments the mandem have nowhere to turn except to people like Leanne, who can lend a listening ear and offer emotional support. Women, often mothers like Leanne, bear the burden and are left to pick up the pieces. They take on a nurturing role with compassion and resilience, providing comfort and understanding when needed, all the while battling their own challenges.

Back inside, Fraser is calmer and chuckles as Leanne encourages him to dance. She swings her hips to the calming sound of Bob Marley and the Wailers' 'Natural Mystic', its reggae beat filling the room like a heartbeat.

'Come on, Auntie Leanne. You know I have no rhythm,' he protests. His movements are awkward and uncoordinated, but that doesn't bother him. He just enjoys the moment, dancing with Leanne as if they're the only ones in the room.

Aron and Cassius burst into laughter at Fraser's dancing.

'Come on, guys! Join us!' Leanne calls, reaching out for Cassius's hand.

When the music shifts to the lively sound of nineties rare grooves, Cassius jumps in.

'No one can test me,' Cassius boasts, grinning as he shows off his moves.

Cassius runs over to me, pulling me on to the dance floor. We burst out laughing as he spins me round.

'I can't remember the last time I laughed this hard. Being at Leanne's just makes me forget about all the bullshit on road. I don't have to be on guard or watch my back. Sometimes, man just needs to let go and feel normal,' Cassius says as he spins me for the third and final time, his laughter ringing out over the music.

It's refreshing to see Cassius let go and have fun. Watching him laugh – his deep, full-body chuckle that comes from a place of genuine happiness – makes me think about how freeing that must feel. Being on road can be risky and isolating, making it hard to relax as you constantly watch your back. Simple pleasures, like joking around and vibing to music – things that many of us take for granted – are incredibly precious for the mandem. In this moment, I see Cassius isn't in survival mode; he's fully alive, embracing every second. This is how life should be lived, but sadly it often isn't. These unguarded moments of pure joy are far too rare, and I can't help but admire this beautiful scene, which, although it should be normal, feels quite extraordinary.

'Where you at, Auntie Leanne? I love you, man,' Cassius yells over the music, stumbling and collapsing drunkenly on the sofa.

Over time, I learned why Aron's friends spent so much time at this place. The truth was that the Cotch provided something of an antidote to the harsh and uncompromising neighbourhood they often struggled to navigate. As I watch Leanne rummage through the cupboard for party games to make them feel like children again, fuss over whether there is enough food for everyone and constantly check if Aron's friends are comfortable, it dawns on me how determined she is to give Aron and his friends a taste of ordinary life. Despite the daily challenges of living in the hood, she pushes on, creating a sense of happiness and peace for those around her. This is especially clear when, despite the incident with Fraser, she refuses to let it ruin the night. The party inside the house goes on as if nothing has happened.

As I enter the kitchen, I smell the sweet scent of freshly baked cake. Leanne is preparing for our second attempt at singing 'Happy Birthday' to Aron, after our first try was interrupted by the incident with Fraser.

'How are you doing, Leanne?' I ask, watching her fuss over Aron's birthday cake, carefully positioning the candles and placing a bright sparkler on top.

'I'm doing great! I'm just so happy that everyone is having such a good time,' she replies, a bright smile lighting up her face.

'Even Fraser seems to have calmed down now. I can't quite put my finger on what's bothering that boy, but I'm relieved he's with us tonight. He's staying over, and I'm going to make sure he has a nice bowl of cornmeal porridge in the morning and wash those filthy tracksuits of his,' she adds with a chuckle, reaching into the cupboard to pull out her camera, ready to capture these joyful memories.

Just then, Cassius strides into the kitchen with a grin spread across his face. 'Are you ready to sing "Happy Birthday", Auntie Leanne?' he asks.

'Come here. Give an old lady a hug!' Leanne says, opening her arms wide as she draws him in. The two share a cherished moment, her arms wrapping tightly round him as she whispers, 'I'm so glad you're all here with me, safe and happy.'

I've always considered Leanne's front door as the

boundary between two completely different worlds. Inside, there's family, normality, and togetherness; outside, danger and death. When the mandem cross this threshold and leave the roads behind, they can drop the facade expected of them. Free to embrace the human moments around them, they are allowed to exist outside the violence that defines their daily lives. The Cotch is a portal – from the public realm to the private one. It's a space of play, love, freedom, and abundance, where they feel safe enough to share their fears, emotional scars, and latent humanity - sides of themselves otherwise hidden from the world. This is where facades fall away, and pure humanity shines through. The playful, joyful interactions at Leanne's house allow them to momentarily shed their on-road identities and embrace a lighter, more carefree version of themselves.

In reflecting on the safety Leanne offers, Bakhtin's concept of 'carnival' comes to mind.[5] He argues that the medieval carnival temporarily liberates people from the oppressive structures of daily life, providing a 'second life' where joy and play prevail, unlocking new possibilities. In this space, social hierarchies are overturned, making way for reinvention. Similarly, Leanne's home becomes a 'second life' for the mandem, a refuge where the rules and pressures of the streets no longer apply. However, Bakhtin reminds us that this respite is temporary. Just as the freedom of the carnival fades and the demands of official order resurface, the pressures of the roads never truly vanish, lurking in the background, ready to steal the fleeting moments of peace.

The crowd begins singing 'Happy Birthday' to Aron just after 11 p.m., but he slips out of the living room, avoiding the moment. I follow him to the dining room and find him standing alone, looking unusually sad. His shoulders are slightly hunched, and his eyes are filled with emotion as he tries to gather himself, clearly lost in thought. Just then, Fraser walks in, sensing immediately that Aron needs some support.

'Bring it in, my G. I miss Dilly too,' Fraser says, reaching out. In a tender moment, he leans in and gives Aron a hug.

As we talk, Aron's dislike for his birthday becomes clear. He shares that, around this time, three years ago, he lost one of his closest friends, Dilly, to gun violence – someone he'd known since primary school and with whom he spent nearly every day.

'I miss him, man,' Aron says. 'I woke up feeling lost today. I visited him, poured some champs on his headstone and spoke to him for hours. I just sat there, not knowing what else to do.' He takes a deep breath before continuing, 'I just can't hold on to joy. I keep thinking about how someone could be here one day and gone the next. I keep thinking that me or one of the other mandem is gonna die next.'

Aron hadn't known the gut-wrenching feeling of being knocked to his knees by a phone call saying his boy had died until he received a call from Cassius. Unsure whether he'd heard the words correctly, he had to ask Cassius to repeat himself over ten times. After hanging up he lay in the dark for weeks, barely speaking and rarely eating. Leanne was so worried about him that she even called his dad, Ray, to whom she only spoke in emergencies. Not even Ray could convince Aron to get out of bed. It was Bella who sat with him every day, eventually convincing him that his life was worth living.

Aron and I sit at the dining room table for hours, watching the guests leave one by one, as we talk about the grief he still carries from losing his friend. He rolls a spliff and pours himself a rum and coke.

'Do you think about death a lot?' he asks, confusion in his eyes as he leans forward, the glass trembling in his hand.

'I just feel anxious all the time. Mum said I need to see a doctor because I'm paranoid. I haven't told anyone this before, but I feel strange; I feel numb.' He runs his thumb along the edge of his glass.

'Half the time, I don't even wanna chill with the mandem or Mumzy. I feel like a black cloud is following me everywhere I go, and I can't get rid of it. I don't have any energy. What do they call it? That get-up-and-go? I'm struggling. Sometimes, I don't even see the point of life.' He stares blankly out of the dining-room window.

'Do you think it's okay for me to think like this? Maybe I'm depressed,' he says.

I try to reassure Aron that his feelings are normal, searching for the right words to comfort him in this vulnerable moment. He takes another sip of his brandy and Coke, the ice clinking softly in the glass. He breathes in deeply, then exhales slowly, as though the words to follow are being dragged from a heavy place.

'I don't wanna end up like Dilly. Mum and Bella tell me I'm only young and life won't always be like this, but I can't believe them because I don't see a way out. I'm in way too deep now. I feel trapped, living on the edge all the time, and it is starting to mess with my head.' He rests his hands lightly against his forehead, as if trying to steady a complicated thought.

'Last week, I couldn't even sleep. I swear I could smell Dilly. I feel his presence like he's hovering over my bed. It's fucking man up. I'm always drenched in sweat when I wake up; the nightmares are the worst.'

The death of close friends is a common experience for young men who live in Northville and other inner-city communities, and they become accustomed to the loss of lives around them. So many young people anticipate an early death and live as if they are dying. They start to care less about the future and the well-being of their future selves, resigned to the harsh reality that surrounds them. Living preciously takes its toll on the mandem. Having people die all around you can only be swallowed so many times before it damages you. The death of Dilly and the lasting trauma paint a distressing picture of the darker side of being on road. Yet the aftermath is rarely acknowledged. Instead, what is too easily lost in the media's portrayal and moral panic over youth violence is the human cost, the pain, the grief, the brokenness that never makes the headlines.

Aron and I head back to the living room as I prepare to say my goodbyes to Cassius and Fraser, the last two people in the house.

Cassius hands Aron a spliff and turns up the volume until the deep, rhythmic beat of Mavado's 'Gully Side' blares through the room. We can't help but sway our heads in perfect harmony, lost in Dilly's favourite song of all time.

'Fraser, big man, go get the Ludi board. Man is here for a bit,' Cassius calls out, his voice rising above the music. 'Aron, pull up a chair. You know we got you, innit? Man is here,' he adds, turning to Aron with the warmest smile, which speaks volumes about their friendship.

Aron responds with a quick fist spud just as Fraser rushes in with the Ludi board. In his other hand, he balances a plate piled high with pieces of fried chicken, eagerly offering it to Aron.

'Tuck into in this, my bro,' Fraser urges.

As I step out of the Cotch around 2 a.m., I leave behind the trio completely absorbed in their lively game of Ludi, their laughter fading into the stillness of the night. The streets are quiet, but my mind is bubbling with thoughts about the time we spent together.

Walking into Leanne's house felt like receiving a warm hug; it was a cosy space that welcomed everyone just as they were, free from any worries or pressure. Inside, it felt as if we were all bound together by an invisible thread, part of something meaningful. Each person brought their own stories and challenges to share, but in this caring environment everyone focused on enjoying the moment without worrying about being judged. Leanne had a special gift for making everyone feel valued, and it was no surprise that the mandem found solace in her home – where a rare sense of peace and renewal, helped lift one another's spirits.

The gatherings at Leanne were about much more than passing the time; they became cherished experiences that highlighted the beauty of genuine human connections. In a world that can sometimes feel overwhelming, Leanne's home stood as a shining example of warmth and community support. It showed that even the heaviest burdens can feel a little lighter when shared with friends and family.

CHAPTER 2

Block

It has been several days since Aron's surprise birthday party, and now I'm chilling with the mandem on a Friday afternoon in a spot they call 'the block'. This term is commonly used to describe a place where friends gather in inner-city neighbourhoods. It's where they pass the time during the day, catch up, buss jokes, bun spliffs and celebrate special occasions. The block is on a residential street, just outside Robbie's home in Northville.

Robbie is an elder in his late fifties, known as the real-life Peter Pan for his refusal to grow up. Interacting with him is always a nightmare, as he's constantly striving to showcase his masculinity, often in absurd ways. Today, he is wearing a colourful string vest that clings to his slim frame, and he's flexing his muscles dramatically in the hopes of gaining attention. Despite his antics, no one else seems to notice him. I can't help but roll my eyes at his constant foolery; it's frustrating and entertaining to watch how hard he tries to be noticed, completely oblivious to the indifference from the mandem and me.

At first glance, the street looks pretty ordinary, with rows of identical brick houses topped with dark grey roofs. But the block is far from typical. It has a lively vibe that takes me back to the old Frontline, though with a lighter, more cheerful energy. Here, the mix of laughter and conversation amidst the daily hustle creates a friendlier atmosphere that was missing from the original Frontline. The block has a vibrant social life, where the mandem come together, enjoying a strong sense of unity and togetherness.

Today, the block is teeming; the atmosphere is festive as the familiar crowd of Adam, Aron, Cassius, and Yardie, Cassius's uncle, plus others I don't recognize, are all present. Everyone is in high spirits, celebrating Yardie's arrival in England. Giggs's 'Talkin da Hardest' blares from Robbie's bedroom window, while champagne is poured, and the aroma of mersh – cannabis – and Robbie's mother's bone-sucking oxtail, which she has been cooking since the morning, fills the air. Everyone indulges in the crates of rum Yardie brought with him from Jamaica. His nickname is Black Santa, because he never arrives in England empty-handed, and his generosity knows no bounds – always bringing alcohol, weed or clothes to the community when he's here.

Robbie and Yardie have just started arguing. Robbie is complaining that Yardie forgot to bring something for him from Jamaica. In his fakest Jamaican accent, he accuses Yardie, 'What you forget 'bout bringing something for the general?'

Yardie responds angrily, 'Ah wah di bloodclart? Wah do dis bredda? General, which part? Why me fi bring tings for you as a big man, me bring tings for the yout dem.' He takes the bottle of rum from Robbie's hand when he's finished speaking.

'Come off my block!' Robbie yells at Yardie.

Before things escalate, Aron steps in to calm things down. 'Relax, my bro,' he says to Robbie. 'Go over there and settle yourself. Cassius, pour this fool a drink before I wild out on him.'

Aron guides Robbie away from Yardie and towards Cassius, sitting in his car.

Robbie likes to think he's the commanding general of the block. Cassius says he behaves like the boss because of his past reputation as a famous drug dealer, known for his expertise in selling hash and making a lot of money. But, these days, people consider Robbie a has-been, broke and struggling financially, and Aron always puts him in his place when he steps out of line. Robbie is forever lecturing anyone who will listen about the thousands of pounds he supposedly has in the bank, though no one believes him. The rumour is that he spends half of his jobseeker's allowance in the bookies, trying to hit a big jackpot, and the other half on wine and spirits to drown his sorrows.

Robbie is also known for his inappropriate behaviour around women. He often catcalls at young girls as they walk past the block. Robbie's cousin, Loretta, now in her sixties, is always the first to call him out and express disapproval. At this moment, she's shouting, 'Dutty ole man!' as she spots Robbie calling out to Gina, a college student, who's walking quickly past us to avoid him. I catch a glimpse of the curtains twitching as Loretta tries to spy on us without being seen. She quickly moves between windows in the house to watch the people outside. If you're fast enough, you might catch a flash of her bleached-blonde hair as she does this. Sometimes she waves at us before quickly hiding again. She keeps an eye on everything, never staying far from the window. Nothing gets past Loretta; she has no filter and tells it like it is.

Lost in the labyrinth of her mind, Loretta has lived as a recluse for most of her adult life, too afraid to leave the home she shares with Robbie and his mother, Matilda. Robbie once mentioned in one of his long lectures that something traumatic happened in Loretta's childhood, something that affected her deeply, though he shows little empathy towards his cousin. Most mornings, Loretta's voice can be heard yelling profanities. In the evenings, she becomes fixated on threatening to throw hot water at the people outside. I'm just hoping she doesn't do it today.

It's so humid outside that Adam has taken off his shirt to expose the tattoo on his chest, which glistens in the sun. He wipes his carefully sculpted six-pack with his purple bandana as he flags down Mr C, the local ice-cream man, who has turned on his jingles to attract the neighbourhood kids. Mr C drives quickly down Kurt Street in his colourful truck.

Adam is five foot five and might be small in stature, but he has the physique of a Greek god, which makes him appear strong and confident. We all know, though, that his appearance is just a facade, and he uses his muscles to mask his shyness and fear of being victimized by rivals. Adam has made it clear to all of us that he hits the gym seven days a week to get strong and avoid threats coming his way. Over the years, I've watched him stick to a strict diet of whole foods and carry a protein shake every single day – without fail. This dedication is both a source of amusement and silent envy among his friends, because, although they would never admit it, they all want to be as fit as Adam. Working out makes Adam feel strong, even invincible, but Cassius has a knack for bringing Adam back down to earth, always reminding him that 'bullets don't discriminate', and that, despite his physique, he, just like any of their friends, 'can get his headback licked off real quick'.

Adam leans against Cassius's car, watching as Cassius excitedly eyes Little Remi. Little Remi at just eleven years old is already taller than most kids his age. He is happily caught up in a water fight with his friends across the street from Robbie's house, skilfully dodging them, laughing and having fun. Cassius decides to join the game, and soon they're all racing towards Arc Park, a local spot famous for the Monkey Tree. This tree has been part of a local folktale since we were kids. Some locals believe it's cursed; they say if you stand directly under it and shout 'stupid monkey tree' three times you'll be jinxed for life.

Cassius has his own reasons for being wary of the tree. He blames it for all his bad luck – from his break-up with Lydia, the first girl he truly loved, to his overall accident-prone nature. Little Remi cleverly leads Cassius close to the Monkey Tree, fully aware that he is afraid of it and avoids it at all costs, calling it the 'Voodoo Tree'. Eventually, Cassius gives up the chase outside the iron railings by the communal green area, realizing Little Remi is employing tactics to take him closer to the tree.

'You're a little dickhead,' he yells jokingly.

Little Remi responds with a mischievous grin, sticking his middle finger up at him.

Used to this commotion and playfulness around her, Mrs Paula, who lives next door to Robbie, happily waters her bright daisies in the hanging baskets by her front door. You can easily spot her by her bright red lipstick and the colourful headwrap that keeps her Afro neat. As she tends to her plants, she sings and hums, something everyone's used to and enjoys. Her husband, Sidney, comes outside to help set up the Ludi table by their front gate and calls over to their neighbour Charlie, inviting him to join them. Charlie is content in his favourite deck chair, with a glass of rum, watching his grandchildren play tag, their laughter echoing down the street as they run around.

The summer season brings the neighbourhood to life. Despite the chaos, Northville still radiates a unique beauty and a proud community spirit. The vibrancy and individuality of each neighbour add a special touch to the surroundings. Sometimes, it's easy to forget that Northville has a lighter side, especially at night when all you can hear are police sirens or helicopters circling the estate. But, if you take a moment to look past all the noise and commotion, you'll see these intimate moments unfolding on the streets: Mrs Paula, Sidney, Charlie and others dancing on their front steps; teenagers playing cards and laughing; kids caught up in kerby or knockdown ginger. You'll see the community coming together in tough times, like when Charlie's wife unexpectedly passed away last year. William, the local priest, recited prayers in the open while neighbours leaned in to grieve with the family. It was the community who rallied around Charlie, ensuring the family was fed and watered for nine nights and the days after. Failing to recognize the underlying humanity and sense of unity here – how people from all walks of life coexist and hold each other together – does a disservice to the 'decent families'[1] that live in Northville, who may have problems, stresses and strains, but otherwise lead peaceful lives.

It's just past 3 p.m., and Adam and Danny – Cassius's younger cousin – are in the middle of their usual heated debate. Adam, with a mischievous grin, waves wads of cash in Danny's face. This argument quickly turns into a battle over who holds the title of the biggest baller (money man) in Northville.

'How much money have you made this week?' Adam enquires, smirking as he faces Danny. 'You're always gonna hate, cos man is a hot stepper out here. I'm better than you, and you know it,' he boasts. 'You're bruk, bruv. You don't make no P.'

Adam is infamous for bragging about his earnings from selling drugs and for flaunting his expensive lifestyle. He even walks into Vinnie's corner shop dressed immaculately – a diamond chain hanging over his carefully ironed shirt – just to buy a carton of milk. He never lets anyone in the community catch him looking off and is determined to maintain the facade of success. His dynamic with Danny has become a familiar spectacle, with Adam constantly belittling him in front of the group. While the clashes get heated, no one takes Adam's outbursts to heart. The mandem brush off his belief that they're jealous of him, with Cassius often shouting that he's 'just a bait drug dealer with way too much to prove'.

Adam boasts about his new Rolex watch he purchased from Hatton Garden that morning. Admiring himself in the reflection of Aron's car window, he liberally applies aftershave and combs his already flawless slicked-back brown hair. True to form, Adam is dressed to impress, sporting diamond grillz on his teeth, a fresh pair of white Air Force 1s, and a Louis Vuitton belt securing his Gucci denim trousers.

With an air of superiority, he turns his boasting in the direction of Little Remi and their friends. 'You young ones need to get your Ps up and jump on the road ting.' He switches his attack back to Danny. 'Bruv, you'll never get one of these in your lifetime,' he says, pointing at his Rolex watch.

This behaviour isn't unique to Adam; it's common among men who grow up in underprivileged urban areas and experience what criminologists refer to as 'relative deprivation'.[2] Popularized by Jock Young and John Lea in the 1980s, the term describes how perceived inequality and social comparison can breed frustration and resentment, which, under certain conditions may lead to criminal behaviour. Young boys and men from low-income backgrounds are often acutely aware of the stark contrast between their lives and the seemingly glamorous lifestyles of others. This awareness fuels a strong desire to project an image of wealth and success, even when the reality is very different. They work hard to maintain the impression that they're not suffering or poor but are, instead, living luxuriously. They build reputations as ballers, 'flossing' – showing off – expensive luxury goods like cars, clothes and jewellery, and adopting identities associated with affluence to gain hood fame and social clout. This image protects them from the emotional toll of their actual circumstances, shielding them from the vulnerabilities of their true selves and marginal status in society – that is, a lack of value and power. By projecting this perceived ideal consumer identity, mandem who cannot access traditional forms of capital can instead obtain 'street capital', a term coined by Sveinung Sandberg in 2008.[3]

In small, tightly knit communities, where everyone knows each other, people are overly concerned about what others own, and those who don't partake in the lifestyle are often harshly judged, labelled a 'waste' and deemed unworthy of respect. For Adam, showcasing his wealth is not just a shield for his insecurities; it also protects him from the inevitable judgement of the wider community. Like Danny, who was judged harshly by Adam, I, too, felt the strong sting of someone flaunting their status.

One day, while waiting for the bus to go to college, Stevie pulled up beside me in his lavish Mercedes. Everyone in our estate saw him as the ultimate success story, and he wore that title of 'baller' with pride. He leaned back in his seat, looked at me through the tinted windows and smirked. Then he criticized me for not owning a car and offered to give me a ride before speeding off, leaving me feeling small and ashamed. After that incident, I would habitually hide behind a metal pole at the bus stop to avoid being spotted by him, or anyone else in the community.

It took almost a decade to unpack the confusing feelings that Stevie's words stirred up in me. I eventually realized I had internalized Northville's narrow definition of success, one dictated by outward appearances and superficial markers, where worth is measured by the car you drive, the designer brands you wear, how flashy you look, how visibly you're seen 'flossing' – and the persistent sense of inadequacy you feel when falling short of this glossy ideal.

It wasn't until I stepped outside the familiar streets of Northville – immersing myself in new environments and engaging with people who held broader, more diverse views on success – that I began to break free from the narrow definition of accomplishment that had been ingrained in the community in which I grew up. I started to define success in a way that felt personal and meaningful, recognizing it as a journey towards contentment and fulfilment, one that looks different for everyone. As I grew older, Northville's idea of success began to seem hollow, a thin disguise, masking deeper truths about self-worth.

Years later, I ran into Stevie again, but this time he zoomed by on a humble electric scooter – a sharp contrast to the flashy lifestyle he used to flaunt. I later learned that the expensive cars he showed off during the summer were actually rentals; he didn't own any of them. They were just props for the image he wanted to create.

Although I have let go of some of these ingrained ideals about looks and status, I must confess that some still stick with me. Sometimes, I get too focused on my appearance - obsessing over buying the latest exclusive trainers like the mandem do, wanting a new shiny diamond ring on my finger, and making sure my hair always looks perfect.

But then there are days when I walk into Vinnie's with messy hair tucked under a New Era cap, deliberately ignoring the pressure to keep up appearances. Maybe it's a small rebellion against those expectations that still weigh on me now and then. Sadly, many people in the neighbourhood still feel trapped in this mindset, convinced that material possessions and the art of impression management are the keys to earning respect and social status.

The fixation on appearing affluent and successful is not limited to specific lifestyles or social classes. Instead, it is deeply ingrained in popular culture. Every day we are inundated with images of the 'good life', especially on social-media platforms that thrive on visual storytelling. A 2024 article by Bill Sullivan in *Psychology Today*[4] discusses how social media can foster a 'stressful materialistic mindset'. For example, on Instagram, people often feel validated by the number of 'likes' and 'followers' they receive, which tends to reward those who flamboyantly display their wealth. This desire to project a glamorous lifestyle influences individual behaviour and societal norms, reshaping our perceptions of success. Unsurprisingly, these pressures are especially strong in urban environments, where the underlying goal remains consistent: to appear successful and earn validation, acceptance and admiration from others. In Northville, the desire to project social status through material possessions is prioritized above all else.

Adam is obsessed with materialism and relentlessly pursues the 'Queen's heads', and the respect that comes with having money. He revels in the spotlight, craving admiration from others, but his behaviour creates tension, especially with Aron.

As Adam soaks up the attention from Little Remi and his friends, Aron glares, barely containing his anger. Before Adam can say anything else, Aron grabs him by the throat and pins him against the concrete wall outside Robbie's house.

'Are you mad, bruv? They are youts. What's wrong with you, my G? Didn't I tell you not to talk about the roads in front of little man?' Aron shouts.

Adam's eyes nervously dart to the ground, too scared to meet Aron's angry face.

'Allow him, man. It's not that deep,' Little Remi pleads, gently gripping Aron's arm to diffuse his escalating anger. But it's a futile effort. Aron is already too wound up to be calmed down.

'I-I don't mean any disrespect, my brudda,' Adam stammers, shifting his weight from one foot to the other. Fear courses through him, knowing he has crossed a line.

'I won't chat to Little Remi again – I swear. Won't say

nothing about the roads to him again,' Adam pleads as he glances up in hopes of a sign of mercy.

'Just know man will buss your head, if you chat shit to him again,' Aron warns, his expression softening slightly as he finally steps back, allowing Adam to go.

Aron has been protective of Little Remi ever since his older brother, Teeky, was sentenced to six years in prison. Stepping in as a surrogate older brother, Aron takes the responsibility to heart. Before Teeky went away, he and Aron were inseparable. Aron promised to look after Little Remi – a vow he holds with deep conviction.

He tries to educate Little Remi about the dangers of being on road, sharing his own cautionary stories to pass on his wisdom. Little Remi was only seven when Teeky was locked up, but he's grown up aware of his older brother's status in the neighbourhood, obvious from the respect shown to him by the young boys on the estate. Little Remi is well aware that Teeky and Aron's reputation protects him, and he sometimes tests the boundaries. Aron's influence is clear: he once reprimanded Little Remi for disrespecting kids at his primary school because of the postcodes in which they live. His school dinner lady reported that he would shout 'Northville soldiers' during his lunch breaks, a behaviour Aron has been working hard to correct. Aron encourages Little Remi to explore new hobbies, like football, taking him to practice on some Sundays when he can. Little Remi often drags his feet to these sessions, only agreeing to go to avoid disappointing Aron.

Little Remi's growing interest in repping his endz is not surprising, but it presents a serious challenge for Aron. He's determined to shield Little Remi from the same fate he faced.

He knows too well the devastating consequences of getting caught up in postcode wars – a relentless cycle of violence that's shaped his choices and limited his future. But the reality is, the postcode wars in Northville have a deep-rooted history, extending over decades – far beyond Aron's control. Young boys growing up here are inevitably drawn into this intergenerational conflict, built by elders who are now either dead or in prison. Tragically, young boys like Aron and Little Remi are born into a cycle of territorial disputes within their own neighbourhoods, a cycle they struggle to fully comprehend. They hold a deep loyalty to their olders yet often lack the context of the conflict's history. If you were to ask them why they are warring over ghosts of the past, they would be at a loss for a clear answer. But, as they come of age on the estate, they form a strong connection to their physical space and develop a resentment towards outsiders. They learn early on that retaliation is the norm – expected even – for any perceived insult or violation. That's how the desire for revenge grows, and every grudge carries the risk of spiralling into violence.

From Aron's experience of being caught in the crossfire of postcode wars and facing the all-consuming pressures of repping endz and showing loyalty, he understands this is not a choice but a predetermined transition from childhood to adulthood and rightly doesn't want this for Little Remi.

The sun begins to set on this summer evening, as Adam, Robbie, Danny and Cassius wrap up their Ludi game. Yardie is preparing to head back to his brother's house, but before he can leave, Robbie can't resist taking another dig at him. This time, he is winding him up about his defeat in the game. Aron brushes off Robbie's disrespect; his attention is elsewhere. He has a frown on his face, too focused on finding Little Remi, who has gone missing in the lively chaos. Moments ago, Danny's friend Pug called him to warn that the Brick Farm youngers — a rival housing estate — were circulating Northville in a black car.

Just as Aron is about to go look for Little Remi and bring him home, a loud gunshot suddenly goes off from the opposite direction to Robbie's house.

'Where the fuck is little man?' Aron shouts in panic, racing towards the sound of the third bang. We — Cassius, Danny and I — all follow him, and as we turn on to Clarence Street a screeching car tears past. We see Ash stumbling into the wheelie bins outside Mrs Paula's house.

'Ash needs help!' I scream.

Aron sprints towards Ash, who is now lying on the ground, breathing heavily. His grey Nike tracksuit bottoms are soaked in blood. Mrs Paula cries out for someone to call the ambulance and presses a tea towel firmly against his leg to stop the bleeding. A deep shock washes over me, paralysing me. I can't speak. Panic and fear squeeze the air from my lungs. I want to help Mrs Paula, but my hands are shaking. Then I vomit on the kerb.

In just an instant, the happiness we all felt before has disappeared.

Ash begins trembling. 'I can't move my legs. Check my back — it feels hot,' he says in panic before fainting.

'Lift him up, man,' Aron pleads.

Only then do I see the fear catch up with him too; his left leg suddenly buckles, but he quickly regains his composure. Aron and Cassius carefully hook Ash's arms over their shoulders and begin walking towards the Cotch, about five minutes from Mrs Paula's.

Neighbours start to spill out of their houses, drawn by the commotion. But only Aron's neighbour, Big Frank, and his young son Pete, step forward to help. The rest stay behind their gates, watching in silence. Amid the noise and rising tension, Ash's eyes open for a moment, and he whispers his mum's name – 'Fiona'. I watch as his friends stagger under his weight, his legs limp and dragging along the ground. I shout after him that we'll find her, hoping he can hear me, as I call out to Mrs Paula to phone Fiona.

When we arrive at the Cotch, the door swings open, and Leanne comes running out, her complexion ghostly pale. Her house is filled with the comforting aroma of jasmine and sandalwood, making me feel calm. For a moment, I detach from the present, pulled into a memory of my Auntie Angie's house, where she would light incense sticks in the hallway and have me blow them out. It occurs to me that in times of fear it's easy to slip out of reality, to take shelter in memories far removed from the heavy, confusing weight of the present. I close my eyes and focus on my breath. The world outside doesn't stop, but something inside me begins to shift. My mind activates a kind of protective mechanism – I can only describe it as an internal bubble of safety, like stepping behind a wall of soundproof glass. The shouting, the noise, the chaos, it all fades away. My heart starts to slow, and my emotions, once scattered, begin to settle. In this serene inner escape, I find the strength and grounding I need to face the challenges that await me outside.

Suddenly, a piercing cry jolts me back to the carnage before me – Fiona has just arrived.

'Who would do this to my son?' she screams, watching

Ash take shallow breaths as he lies on Leanne's cold kitchen floor.

'We called the ambulance about five minutes ago, Auntie Fiona,' Aron shouts.

As we wait for the ambulance, Fiona holds her son's hand tightly and rocks back and forth, whispering to him, 'I'm sorry, baby. I should have moved you away from all this bullshit time ago.' Then she starts howling as if in pain.

The eerie sound breaks Aron's trancelike state, and he rushes outside to catch his breath. He paces up and down the street, biting his fingernails anxiously, scanning every car that drives past his house. He's yelling on his mobile, 'They aren't getting away with this.' It sounds as if he is plotting a revenge attack. I can hear the ambulance siren in the distance, and it feels like we've been waiting for it to arrive forever. In my moment of panic, I'm convinced that ambulances take longer to come to estates than other addresses. I just hope the delay hasn't put Ash at extra risk. The paramedics jump out, and in minutes Ash is strapped to a stretcher and rushed away.

Shortly after Ash leaves in the ambulance, Aron rounds up Cassius, Danny and Ash's cousin Georgie, who has just arrived. Aron stares at Leanne, before jumping on his push bike, riding away from his mother's house with the mandem in tow, ignoring her calls not to do anything stupid. But it's too late; Aron isn't answering his phone. He, Danny, Cassius and Georgie have ridden out of the estate, deciding to take matters into their own hands. Aron's composure is gone under the stress of the situation, and he's hurt and in pain.

Several days after the incident, I head to the Cotch, determined to check in on Ash and piece together what really happened that day. Each step feels heavy, weighed down by the emotional toll of everything I witnessed. The haunting image of Ash's bloodied body forces me to reflect on the brutality to which their bodies (and souls) can be subjected and how easily they can be hurt by a normalized regime of brutality. Leanne's tearful words from that day echo in my mind: 'The roads are taking our kids, and no one seems to care.' After what I had seen, her words took on a new weight. Neither Leanne nor I knew what Aron would do after holding his wounded friend in his arms. She didn't know if she would see her son again once he rode out of the estate, searching for the people who'd hurt Ash. All she knew was that Aron was in danger, and she had no idea how to protect him. As I walk, a grim realization settles over me: the roads offer no real freedom, no hint of a promising future. This thought transforms my slow, contemplative walk into a run, as I rush to see if Ash is okay.

Running along Donald Street and past Vinnie's, heading towards the traffic lights, I exchange a wave with the old vicar, William, who is talking to Mrs Paula. They both call out to me, smiling. Vicar William is always in deep conversation with members of his church – many seek his counsel and attend his Sunday services faithfully. The mandem tend to steer clear of the church, gravitating towards the local mosque, which always draws a large crowd.

I arrive just as Zak is leaving for work. I step over the 'Home Sweet Home' doormat and head into the living room. There, I find Ash lounging on Leanne's sofa while Aron is completely absorbed in playing *Grand Theft Auto*. Ash hasn't touched the plate of food beside him, but he keeps insisting that Aron finds Georgie. They haven't been in touch since they all left the estate that evening, and now everyone's starting to worry – Georgie isn't answering any calls.

Ash smiles, showing off his bright white teeth, and warmly invites me to sit beside him. I can tell he's in pain, shifting between sitting upright against the sofa and lying down. When he speaks, his voice is soft and hard to hear. I ask how he's doing, and he just shrugs and lets out a sad chuckle.

'I'm fine. I've just been in hibernation since I was shot.' He shakes his head and exhales a deep sigh.

'What happened?' I ask, watching Ash struggle to compose his thoughts, his eyes clouded with confusion.

'I was making my way back from watching my cousin's football match,' he begins, his voice shaking slightly. 'I saw this car creeping down the street, but at first I didn't penny it. Then it circled back, and that's when I realized I was fucked.'

'I started to run, but my legs buckled. Then I heard the shot and felt heat in my back, then my leg. Everything was a blur. Man was in a daze. I kept trying to call Aron, but my hands were sweating.' He takes a deep breath, his gaze distant.

'All I could think was, I need to see my mum, I don't wanna die without saying goodbye, so I kept running, pushing myself to get home. I made it to Mrs Paula's house. After that, I don't remember nothing else,' he says, turning to Aron.

'It's madness, man,' Aron, says, jumping in. 'He didn't see it coming.' There's a sadness in his tone. 'He took the fall for everyone,' he continues.

'What do you mean?' I ask.

Aron's expression changes. 'It could have been any of us who got shot that day. It just so happens that Ash was the first one they spotted. That's how this postcode madness operates; anyone who's known on road can be targeted,' he explains.

'How did this all start?' I press, searching for clarity.

Aron sighs deeply, a moment of silence hanging between us before he speaks.

'It all started with the olders and their beef. Us youngers inherited their problems, their grudges. The boy who shot Ash, we all know him. Georgie went to school with him. This postcode ting divides us. I went to primary school with some of the boys I'm warring with now. We used to walk home together. Our mums and grandparents even attended the same church back in the day.'

'What changed? Why did those connections fade away after primary school?' I ask.

'Secondary school changes everything,' Aron says, his voice low and reflective.

'Why's that?'

'It's hard to explain,' he continues, looking serious as he tries to find the right words.

'Everyone has a different experience. On a reals, it all went left when I got to around Year Nine or Ten, and some youts from Brick Farm rushed me. Imagine, before then, I was friends with the ones who were in my school. We were always getting into trouble with the teachers together.'

'Yeah, it's deep, man,' Ash adds, sharing a meaningful glance with Aron.

'When they violated man, my war with them started. Yeah, we inherit beef from the olders, but my issues with them are personal. Where another man might ride out just because they want to rep Northville and take on the olders' issues, I had to fight back cos man was violated. I am not letting anyone fuck with me and get away with it,' Aron explains, his eyes filled with the weight of his memories.

'Why did they rush you?' I ask, eager to understand the roots of this rivalry.

'When one of their olders got murdered, they weren't having it. It was game on from that point. They were violating anyone they saw from Northville. Things escalated quickly,' Aron replies, shaking his head at the recollection.

'Yeah, the postcode war got serious real quick,' adds Ash. 'We have to sever ties with any man from that estate, and man has to protect our friends. The postcode ting started cos of the history between the olders, but now man is warring over new violations. It's just tit-for-tat. The youngers have their own problems with each other, caught up in their own problems now. This is why it's never gonna end, cos too many man have been violated differently. It's gone past showing loyalty to your endz; it's about being loyal to your boys and riding out when they get touched,' Ash explains, leaving an unsettling silence as I absorb the harsh reality of their world.

I was beginning to understand how loyalty runs deep with the mandem. It wasn't just a word thrown around lightly – it's real, carrying serious consequences. They'll go to extraordinary lengths to stand by one another, risking everything to back their boy. Loyalty in friendship can be a beautiful thing, but in places like Northville, where just getting through the day can wear you down, that same loyalty can shift – becoming dangerous, even destructive. I was starting to see, though, that there was more to it. It carries a weight you don't fully understand until you're right there, in the middle of it, seeing what it really looks like up close. That's what I saw with Aron and Ash. Watching Aron make Ash a hot chocolate every few hours, sort out food for him, and constantly check if he was okay – even when Ash got annoyed – I realized this was more than friendship. It was a brotherhood forged in shared experiences and unspoken trauma.

Because of what they live through together – the shootings, stabbings, mandem murdered before they even have a chance to finish school or simply enjoy being kids – they share a deep and complicated bond. They are willing to go to extreme lengths to protect each other, even if that means picking up a weapon and going down a dark path. In this tangled, bittersweet web of loyalty, their devotion is both touching and tragic – the very friendships that offer strength and support can also become the ties that lead to their downfall.

What struck me the most was how calmly they spoke about the violence that robbed them of the childhood they should have had. It's heartbreaking to see how numb they've become to the hurt and pain, and how early that emotional switch turned off. Yet despite everything, even in their darkest hours, they continue to hold each other down, because, in a life that's already taken so much from them, their loyalty is the last thing they refuse to lose.

Cassius enters the room, looking dazed. His bloodshot eyes and the packet of Wotsits he's munching on leave no doubt he's high. But he's eager to join the conversation and he shares his perspective.

'You know I'm always happy, but since I saw Ash fucked up like that I've been feeling mad different. I'm just getting tired of all this, man. Having to keep riding out.' Cassius sighs, taking another pull from his spliff, exhaustion written across his face.

'Why is it so difficult to change and lead a different life?' I ask.

Cassius shakes his head. 'You make it sound so simple,' he

replies. 'We grew up in these slums; it's not easy living here. If you don't retaliate, then them man will take set on you.'

He leans back against the sofa. 'Ask any of the mandem if they woke up one day and thought, *Yeah, man is gonna be on this postcode ting*. Nah, most mandem will tell you that the hood forces you into this life.'

Cassius pauses, his eyes wide, clearly haunted by recent events. 'But now man is really starting to rethink this road ting. I just want to be happy. I don't wanna keep playing Russian roulette, wondering when it's my turn to get touched next,' he admits. 'Don't get me wrong – we've all been violated somehow, but Ash was the first to be seriously hurt. It's got man thinking if all this shit is really worth the hype,' he says, his tone growing more serious.

'I usually laugh tings off, don't even get emotional, but this . . . this is messed up, man,' Cassius murmurs, shaking his head as he drifts off to the kitchen in search of more snacks.

The doorbell rings unexpectedly, and Aron starts to panic. 'You man, get up quick, man! Open up the window! My mum's back!' he shouts at Ash and Cassius, nearly tripping over the couch in his rush. Leanne has come home from a long shift at the care home and forgotten her front-door keys. Cassius cautiously steps into the hallway, ready to help her with the heavy Asda grocery bags she's struggling to carry.

From the kitchen, Leanne calls out sharply, 'Aron, it's time for your friends to leave – and open the goddamn window. I told you not to smoke that shit in my house. You know what the doctor said about your asthma!'

Cassius and Ash hurry past the kitchen, waving goodbye. 'See you soon, Auntie Leanne!' they shout.

Leanne pauses to take a puff from her cigarette, her face

showing signs of stress as she loads another batch of laundry into the washing machine. She then asks Aron to run to Vinnie's for more cigarettes since she's running low. Now dressed in a crisp white T-shirt, True Religion jeans and Giuseppe trainers, Aron rushes down the stairs to help. As he offers to grab the cigarettes before heading out, Leanne looks puzzled and asks about his plans.

'Relax, Mum,' he reassures her. 'I'm just popping out for a bit.'

Aron and I sit on the front steps as he gets ready to head to Shyanne's for the evening. He pours us brandy and coke into small plastic cups and rolls a spliff. I notice his anxiety in the way his feet tap nervously, so I seize the moment to check in.

'I'm still angry,' he admits. 'I just need a change of scenery to clear my head.' His phone buzzes incessantly beside him, calls he ignores as he keeps talking.

'Seeing Ash so feeble like that made me see red,' he confesses. 'You know I rode down there, not caring who I bukked. All I knew is that someone had to pay for what they did to him. But when man got there it was like a ghost town. They must have known we were coming.'

He takes a deep breath before continuing.

'I just left Georgie there. He said he wasn't giving up. He did an all-night stakeout.'

Aron slumps slightly. 'I'm just drained, man. Mum's drained. Everyone around me is worried, and that just adds to my problems.' There's a shift in his voice when he speaks about Leanne. 'She looks at me with this sad look, always telling me about the days when I was this loving son.' He pauses before adding, 'I remember those days too, but now man is lying to her, taking her money, so she doesn't clock that I sell drugs. I feel shame, but don't know how to live differently.'

'What do you mean by that? Why is it so difficult to leave the roads behind?' I nudge gently, hoping he'll open up.

'You think I don't want to leave? he snaps back, more defensive now. 'I was talking to Cassius the other day and realized man is just scared of life. I don't feel grown up enough. I don't even feel strong enough to manage my own mind. How can I even face the real world?' He shrugs, his eyes low. 'I don't know how to handle that normal civilian life. I didn't finish school, I don't have no work history, I don't have those, uhm, what do you call them . . . social skills to manage out there.'

'Of course you do,' I reply. 'You have plenty of those. You're charismatic and connect with people easily. Everyone loves you.'

'That's a really nice thing to say,' he responds, sounding a bit warmer, but you can still hear the doubt in his voice.

'Even if I could leave the roads, my enemies wouldn't let me. When you have a bait face like mine, when you have violated people, they don't just forget, even if they see you in a suit. They don't care if you've changed, because they haven't.'

Aron pulls a note from his jacket pocket as we sit together, watching Little Remi and his friend play a game of tag. He has written a poem he wants to share. With a proud smile, he begins to recite:

'*I dream of an island so far away. A beautiful life beyond these concrete walls. A life filled with endless possibilities. A world behind a virtual picket fence where you get to choose who you want to be rather than the badman you are destined to be. In this world my dreams are as big as mountains so is my view of the world, I see no barriers or differences between them or I. But in my real world, tortured and lost souls roam free, hearts bleeding, the cycle of violence never ends. In the world behind the virtual picket fence, I have a reason to smile: I've defeated the beast and I am in heaven again!'*

His voice is a little hesitant as he asks, 'What do you think of the poem?'

'It's incredible,' I reply.

Aron's face lights up for a moment as he takes in my words, then begins to share a piece of his past.

'I've always liked poetry. Back in primary school, I'd sit in the corner with felt-tip pens and coloured cards. Green was my favourite colour – it still is – and I would write down my feelings on paper. It helped me understand things better,' he reflects, his voice warm as he recalls his childhood.

He continues, his voice growing more emotional. 'I think I write to cope with life, you know? It's a way to get lost in my imagination. Life is just fucked. I ain't really living. It feels like I'll always be trapped here, waiting for something to change.'

Even though there's sadness in his eyes, there's also a bright spark. His poetry isn't just an escape; it's how he makes sense of everything he carries. It lets him shape his pain into words, and somehow, through that process, he finds a quiet kind of beauty. Every line he writes offers him a breath of something bigger, a moment of freedom, a glimpse of the life of which he can only dream, just beyond the limits of his reality.

As our conversation winds down, Aron hesitantly reaches for his phone, which he has been avoiding since we sat down.

When the screen lights up with Cassius's name, his jaw clenches – as if he's already bracing himself for the worst. He answers the call and listens. There's a long pause. Then he looks up, his gaze distant as he shares the news. After Ash was attacked, Georgie started carrying a gun. He didn't want to be an easy target. But the very next day the police stopped him. Now Georgie is in prison.

Aron speaks to me in a hushed tone, as if saying it too loudly might make the situation feel more real. After a pause, our conversation shifts from Georgie to the harsh reality of living in Northville, where the concept of freedom feels like a mere illusion.

As he heads to the car, he glances back at the estate with a sense of defeat, muttering almost to himself, 'Same shit, different day. You really can't make this shit up.'

He honks the horn to say goodbye and rushes off to meet Cassius, leaving me behind to process the heavy news. Outside, life carries on as usual, but inside the estate it feels like the mandem are trapped in a perpetual bad dream. With Georgie locked up, and Aron stuck wondering if this is all there is, it's a harsh reminder that they are merely surviving, while the rest of the world gets to truly live.

CHAPTER 3

Shubs

I'm waiting outside St Vincent's Church with Cassius, Aron and Fraser. It's a short walk from the block, standing quietly on the corner of the estate. This stone building has been here longer than any of us, surviving the urban regeneration that erased so many familiar landmarks. I can faintly hear Vicar William's voice from inside, rising and falling, just as it did when I was a kid listening to his sermons. We are surrounded by about a hundred people, all gathered to say their final goodbye to Cassius's uncle, Harry. That alone says a lot about who he was. The drummers play in the background. Their rhythm carries something heavy, but it's not quite sadness. It feels like a tribute – a vibrant, heartfelt celebration of his life.

Aron reaches into his coat pocket, pulls out a pair of dark Ray-Bans, and hands them to Cassius. 'You good?' he asks.

Today, Cassius isn't his usual composed self. He's drunk, unsteady and broken in a way that's hard to see. Saying goodbye to the man who meant everything to him isn't just challenging – it feels like everything is falling apart.

Harry wasn't just his uncle; he was a father figure, a mentor, and Cassius's closest friend. He stood by Cassius through the good times and the bad. When things got messy, it was Harry's steady voice that cut through the chaos. He just knew how to ground Cassius when he was spiralling.

At family gatherings, Harry gave the kind of speeches people remembered, especially the one where he proudly 'bigged up' Cassius. He was a peacemaker too. When emotions ran high between Cassius and his mother, Harry was the calm voice of reason.

His love showed up most in the little things, like the meals he cooked with care. Harry's red pea soup was legendary: packed with dumplings, okra, pumpkin, yam and banana. It was more than just food; it was comfort. It was history. It meant Cassius never had to worry about going hungry. Their bond ran deep, built on respect, shared stories and years of showing up for each other. Now, outside the church, Cassius stands beneath the full weight of that loss. The grief presses down on him – a reflection of how much Harry meant to him.

In the warm afternoon sun, the distant melody of Bob Marley's 'Jah Live' ripples through the air, signalling the start of the procession. A polished black hearse gently comes to a stop outside the church. Behind it, Bennie, Harry's neighbour, follows closely, his car stereo booming out a playlist of Harry's favourite tunes. Soon after, a line of thirty cars begins to assemble along the road, each vehicle serving as a tribute to the countless lives Harry had touched. One by one, mourners spill out from their cars, wearing touches of yellow – Harry's favourite colour – in a heartfelt display of love and remembrance.

Cassius rushes towards the hearse, pausing in front of a portrait of his uncle when he was younger. Harry was known for his charm, earning the nickname Casanova, a title he carried with him until his passing at sixty.

As Cassius gazes at the familiar face in the photo, Aron steps closer, and leans in, whispering in his ear, 'It's time, my brudda.'

He guides him towards his five uncles, who are waiting to help carry Harry's casket into the church. The sound of the drums grow louder, and the crowd chants in rhythm as they follow the coffin. Aron stays close to Cassius, watching over him, and when his friend's legs begin to give way he rushes in to steady him.

'I'm good, my G,' Cassius says, his voice filled with determination as he straightens up.

The service opens with a heartfelt mix of hymns and tributes honouring Harry, delivered by his closest family and friends. Cassius stands at the podium, visibly moved, taking in the weight of the moment. His voice trembles as he struggles to express his feelings during the eulogy, tears streaming down his cheeks, partially hidden by his dark sunglasses. Beside him, Vicar William offers quiet words of encouragement and support.

As the service comes to a close, mourners rise and move towards the front of the church to pay their final respects to Harry. His tribute song, Garnett Silk's 'What Do You Say', plays softly in the background. One by one, they bow their heads and step forward, some barely holding it together, others whispering quiet prayers. The open casket is draped in the Jamaican flag – bold, bright and full of pride, just like Harry. Every detail, from the music to the colour scheme, honours him and brings us together, a powerful reminder of the legacy Harry leaves behind.

At the reception following the funeral, guests have been mingling for a while. It's well past 10 p.m., and Cassius is still drinking. Every new guest who arrives keeps topping up his plastic cup, even though it's clear he's had enough.

'Cassius, I think it's time to stop drinking,' I say, with concern.

He ignores me and walks over to Anthony, his godbrother, who has just arrived after missing the morning service and burial. Anthony used to show up for important events, but since moving to South London he hasn't been around much. Anthony, older than the rest of the group and in his thirties, is charismatic, and is using his charm to convince Cassius to come with him to some shubs – a party – south of the river.

Even though Anthony didn't attend the funeral, Cassius is still happy to see him, and pulls him in for a hug. I was surprised when Anthony suggested going out to a party and meeting girls, but not shocked. Anthony tends to cope with tough life events by avoiding them through partying. I remember how, after his cousin's tragic car accident two years ago, he buried his grief in weekends of nightclub life, alcohol and fleeting encounters with women he barely knew. For what felt like an eternity he seemed to operate on autopilot, steering clear of any conversations about loss. Now, he refuses to talk about Harry's passing. But I understand – this is how he copes, hiding his sorrow beneath layers of distraction.

'Yeah, let's goooooooo! Aron, mandem, are you coming?' Cassius says, slurring his words.

I turn to Anthony and give him a cold stare. 'Anthony, are you serious? Look at him. He's not in a fit state to go raving.'

But before I can say another word Cassius cuts me off, shaking his head in annoyance and telling me to calm down.

'Relax. We're not known in South, so we'll be safe.'

Cassius knows that I'm concerned that leaving Northville could be violent. We all know that any potential trouble is more likely to happen in our area where they have beef with people. But, I'm more worried about their eagerness to explore an unfamiliar location when everyone is grieving deeply.

Anthony describes the party he wants to go to – it's a late-night spot inside a Caribbean restaurant, which he and the mandem have dubbed 'the shit shack' because of its shabby decor. According to Anthony, a mix of people frequent it, including older Caribbean men with strong opinions, women who hail from Jamaica (sometimes known as 'yardies'), locals from the estate and more. This is where they all come together most nights.

Under normal circumstances, Cassius would never agree to attend some shubs in South – his safety is always his top priority. He's always been excessively cautious, even when he is sober, but today grief and drink have a stronger influence on him. He has forgotten, or perhaps pushed aside, the many stories we've all heard growing up about fights breaking out at hood raves and how quickly those fights can turn deadly. Just last month, Aron's cousin Giggy was mistakenly shot in his shoulder while waiting in his car outside a local party for his girlfriend. In a moment of chaos, his life could have been easily lost.

Going to a rave in London is a common way for many people to socialize, but, on the estate, heading out can be risky, especially for young men who might react aggressively if they feel their masculinity is being challenged. Because of this, the mandem usually stay close to Northville, avoiding places, people or situations that could put them in active danger.

This caution means they rarely take trips to central London

or visit tourist spots in other boroughs or cities as most people do. It's rare for them to venture out of the endz and explore beyond their comfort zone. Stepping out feels unpredictable, unsafe and unfamiliar. They mostly miss out on what many of us take for granted – the freedom to travel around, explore and enjoy all that London has to offer. Instead, they're often limited to their postcodes, confined to a small, familiar environment.

Even though stepping into new spaces can be anxiety-inducing, the mandem try not to let fear take control of their lives. It's a careful balancing act between staying safe and enjoying life. They seek out these little moments of connection, laughter and fun whenever they can. I guess it's their way of reminding themselves that they're alive, that there is still space for happiness, even when danger is close.

Initially hesitant about the idea of heading to the shubs, I find myself swept along by Cassius, who insists I join them. Before I know it, I'm pulling out of the church-hall car park, driving to South London with Aron, Cassius, Ash and Anthony in my car. The rest of the group follows closely behind us. I can tell I'm not the only one feeling uneasy. Aron, ever the strategist, seems just as concerned and he's planned for the worst-case scenario by bringing along more friends. For him, there is safety in numbers – a principle he adopted after a scary experience last year when he had to escape some rivals by jumping over a fence and hiding in strangers' gardens after leaving his voluntary work placement. Aron vowed he would never travel alone again, and that memory still shapes the way he makes decisions.

Being in a big group can sometimes attract unwanted attention, but for the mandem the thought of being alone feels even more frightening. They often find themselves in a tough spot: go out together and risk being seen as a gang, or go out alone and face potentially dangerous situations. Even in a large and diverse city like this, life can feel quite restrictive. Tensions can rise and boil over when rival groups unexpectedly cross paths, whether it's on a bus, train, at a party or even at the local barbershop.

Aron, like many of his friends, feels this pressure. To stay safe, he surrounds himself with a close-knit group of four or five friends, who provide him a sense of security against unexpected threats. No longer willing to be caught off guard, he 'rolls' with his entourage, feeling more relaxed as we set off into the unpredictable night.

Inside my car, it's pulsing with energy. Anthony, as usual, is being annoying, singing loudly to Method Man's (featuring Mary J. Blige) 'All I Need' at the top of his lungs. Ignoring my request to turn down the car stereo, he turns it up to full blast. He's also paying no attention to my warning about smoking his spliff in the car. The car reeks of pungent skunk, and the air freshener hanging from the rear-view mirror does little to mask the unpleasant stench of sweat and spliff. I'm anxious, shouting at Anthony to put it out before we get pulled over by the police, but, as usual, he's 'hard of hearing' and doesn't listen.

Cassius sticks his head out of the car window, like a dog experiencing new sights and smells for the first time. He's excited, calling out to every person who walks by as I drive. Aron's so high that he's caught the laughing bug and can't stop grinning, while I get annoyed at the satnav for constantly leading me down the wrong road. I'm really irritated by their childish behaviour, especially since Cassius thinks it's a good idea to invite other motorists to join our convoy on the way to the party.

Lost, I pull up beside a man in a suit, sitting in a luxury Range Rover near Clapham Common. Without hesitation, Cassius invites him too. Surprisingly, the businessman humours him by asking for the party's address. Cassius has a unique charm that can impress and disarm anyone. His humility and eagerness to connect with people from all backgrounds are his strongest traits, even though his serious face often leads people to misjudge him at first. But when he breaks into his goofy laugh, those assumptions quickly fade.

Once, an elderly lady clutched her handbag at the sight of him. Cassius asked her straight out if she thought he was a thief. Minutes later, they were walking down the street together – he was carrying her Tesco shopping bags, listening closely as she shared childhood memories of growing up in Pakistan.

We arrive at the shubs shortly after midnight. The venue sits on a quiet street with nothing much else around. The place feels empty and lonely, as if it has been long forgotten. There's a long, winding road, abandoned flats on either side, and cars parked on the kerb, gathering dust. There are no people in sight, just the sound of the wind blowing and streetlamps that flicker on and off. Instantly, I feel alone and start thinking about how dangerous these venues can be. If something were to happen, no one would be around to help. And even if someone was watching from behind their windows we wouldn't see them.

Cassius and Anthony are the first to jump out of my car, rushing into the venue with the excitement of two giddy toddlers. As the West Indian saying goes, 'Alcohol can turn some people fool!' Aron is the opposite – silent and alert. He pulls his coat tight, scanning the street to see if any youts from South might jump out from the shadows. His face says it all; he's looking to leave the venue before we've even stepped inside.

Anthony seems to be oblivious to Aron's growing concern. He is frantically searching the back seat of the car, cursing and blaming Cassius for misplacing his mobile phone. Meanwhile, Aron has moved closer to a tree on the right side of my car. Though it doesn't provide complete cover, I assume he feels safer hiding behind it than being exposed and vulnerable. For now, the tree acts as Aron's safety blanket, but he's becoming increasingly agitated with Anthony, demanding that he finds the phone quickly or else he will leave.

After some searching, Anthony finally spots his phone lying on the passenger-seat floor. We all rush towards the venue, keeping an eye on our surroundings. We enter through the main door into a dimly lit restaurant packed with tables and chairs. From there, we head through a garden area and finally into a back room, where the party is already in full swing.

The shubs is rammed with people, but what catches my attention is how small the place feels, yet, somehow, there's room for a jerk barbecue and four wooden speaker boxes painted in red, gold and green, along with a sound system decorated with pictures and memorabilia of Bob Marley. Meanwhile, on the worn dance floor, a crowd of yardie women are brukking out – letting loose as they do the 'dutty wine'.

A man with a video camera captures the excitement as the women take turns, boasting about how 'pretty and cute' they are, and sharing how many children they have. I've seen this exhibition before. Typically, groups of women dressed to impress try to grab the attention of the cameraman and what's locally known as the 'video light'. They step into the bright spotlight, competing to be noticed in a vibrant display of pageantry and self-expression. They own the dance floor, each woman expressing her individuality through dance, outfits and presence. It's a celebration that feels both personal and unapologetic.

Walking through the large, sweaty crowd, I spot a girl in a Lycra catsuit and pink high heels. She catches the cameraman's attention as she slow wines down to the floor, moving her bum into a flick. The camera light is bright and blinding, but I can still see the girl reach her hands back and grab hold of Aron, bending right over so that her bum is touching his crotch.

Aron is not impressed and amps up, 'What is this mad gal on?' He desperately tries to escape the video light and the growing crowd gathered around them. I can't help but chuckle – he's so antisocial. Suddenly, Cassius runs over to us, mocking Aron, and says, 'Isn't that Shanilay, bro?' Aron does a double take and replies, 'Wow, it really is her! She looks mad different, bro,' almost choking on his bottle of Magnum. Aron just realized that the girl who wined on him was his childhood friend Shanny, short for Shanilay. Aron, still surprised at Shanny's transformation, takes pictures of her for evidence. Shanny seems to enjoy the attention she's getting from him. During the day, she is shy and reserved, going to college and keeping her head down. Here, she is confident, dressed sensually and in her element.

Hood raves are unique spaces where young women and men can let go and become someone else for the night. They carry a different energy – almost like red-carpet events for women, creating an opportunity for them to shine like glamorous stars. It's inspiring to see women like Shanny – often invisible – become visible and empowered by their defiant style and sensuality. This is their playground, not just a space to be seen, but admired, even celebrated, if only for a night.

Shanny revels in the music, grabbing Cassius, who is skanking in the middle of the dancefloor, and she starts daggering him. The crowd cheers and sings along to Wayne Wonder's 'Anything Goes' blasting through the speakers in each corner of the room. The bass hits so hard I feel it vibrating through my body.

The ragga music has completely captivated the crowd. To my left, the mandem from South move in sync to Vybz Kartel's infectious track 'Clarks'. They proudly tap their stylish suede Clarks boots as they stomp to the bass, waving Jamaican flags and blowing neon-coloured woofer horns. And to my right Cassius impresses two women with his extravagant dancing: he's gyrating his hips, drawing closer to one of the women, holding her waist to start slow-wining. He mistakenly thought he could take on these ladies, but they sandwich him, wining, bum-flicking and having fun at his expense – he doesn't stand a chance!

As the DJ turns up the music to the max, it's as if I'm suddenly in the middle of the lively streets of Kingston. The sound system hits hard, and the energy is impossible to ignore. In Jamaica, sound systems and street parties aren't just events – they're part of how the community lives and connects. The tradition began in the late 1940s, when sound systems brought joy and a respite from the everyday struggles people faced in their communities. They were more than music; they symbolized hope. As cultural historian Norman Stolzoff[1] highlights in his 2000 book, *Wake the Town and Tell the People*, these gatherings are important beyond entertainment. They provide vital spaces for empowerment and resistance where marginalized voices unite and find strength.

As I stand in the shubs tonight, soaking in the good energy and the ragga music pulsing though the room, I can't help but reflect on how far Jamaican culture has travelled beyond the island. There's a real feeling of freedom in the air – people are skanking, laughing, vibing without holding back. It hits me how open and comfortable everyone seems here.

I see Cassius enjoying himself, smiling widely. I grab his hand and shout over the music, 'How are you feeling? Are you okay?'

He puts both hands on my shoulders. 'I needed this, man. If only Uncle Harry could see me now.' He stands still before walking back into the lively crowd of dancing people. His grief has lifted for a moment. Here, he's found peace – dancing and floating around without a care in the world.

Even I'm caught up in the good vibes at the shubs, and my earlier fears and reservations fade as the DJ changes pace from ragga to R&B. When my favourite track, 'Can't You See' by the classic group Total, comes on, I can't help but dance – it's one of those old-school bangers you just have to jam to no matter where you are.

Every time I hear it, I'm instantly transported back to childhood, to those endless, carefree summer days hanging out on the estate. Back then, Lorrie, Neva and I would slick our bangs to our foreheads with gel – which caused plenty of facial acne. We loved rocking big chunky gold hoop earrings and matching chaps chains, trying to capture Aaliyah's attitude and iconic style. Even though my dance moves have become a little rusty over the years, this song has me feeling and dancing like I'm back in the late nineties all over again.

As the music shifts back to bashment, the DJ gives a special shout out to Anthony, who stands surrounded by his friends from his new endz. Anthony is well known around here. Since relocating to South London a couple of years ago, he quickly made connections and learned how things worked in the area, figuring out who holds power and influence. This ability to fit in and thrive also earned him respect in Northville.

Anthony opens a bottle of champagne, and raises it high, inviting Aron and the rest of our group to join him. With a wide grin, he introduces us to his friends, generously topping up everyone's plastic cups with alcohol.

SK, a small, slim young man with a deep, unique voice, introduces himself to us first. He stands next to two older mixed-race women who look excited and tired at the same time. Cigarettes dangle from their mouths and they seem high on something more potent than marijuana. They look straight past me and scan the mandem, staring at Aron and Ash, winking at them and pulling down their tops to show a little more cleavage.

'These light-skinned tings best not even look my way. They think they're so nice,' Ash declares loudly. Aron looks at me with a raised eyebrow and seems just as embarrassed as I am right now.

Cassius ignores the fact that SK has hailed him up and decides to introduce himself to one of his female guests instead.

'Girl, you're pretty.' He takes her hand and spins her round. She smiles, flattered. Cassius's eyes pop out of his head as he whispers to Aron that 'this lightie [a person of mixed-race heritage] has a back off'.

Aron pushes him away. 'What's wrong with you, blud? What a fucking gal clown?'

Aron and Cassius regularly argue about how Cassius views and treats women. Cassius is currently with his partner, Jackie, but Aron doesn't like hearing him brag about being unfaithful. Just last month, Cassius was obsessed with an Italian girl called Sofia, whom he met at Anthony's kid's christening. Two weeks ago, he was smitten with a girl called Pretti, from the same christening, and this week he's been wining and dining (at Nando's) a girl he met from Portugal.

It's a little past 2 a.m. when I check my phone while standing in line for some jerk chicken and hard food. The line is long and full of drunk, rowdy and hungry people. As I wait, Ash starts sharing his story on Snapchat, excitedly telling his followers where he's partying tonight. Just as he is about to reveal the location, Aron snatches his phone and interrupts him.

'Turn that shit off. Are you mad, bruv? Why are you hotting man up?' I watch Aron reprimand Ash for his reckless behaviour and notice a partygoer walking cautiously towards us, his gaze fixed on Aron. The man stands beside him, grinning, gripping a bottle of Guinness and humming along to Jah Cure's 'Western Region'. He speaks only to Aron.

'What's wrong, my yout? Nah budda go to your yard. The party nah go be the same without you,' he jokes, trying to lighten the mood. He must have overheard Aron saying he was planning to leave this 'dead shubs'. From the moment we arrived, Aron has been complaining about wanting to leave. He isn't feeling the vibe, and the unfamiliar faces around us make him even more eager to go.

Before Aron can respond, Dustin – Anthony's right-hand man – aggressively steps towards the man and presses his weight against him.

He barks at him, 'What are you on about? Mind your business. Why are you asking my man questions?'

The man responds with the same intensity. 'Who are you talking to? What? Do you want me to go get my ting?'

The man has made a threat to get his gun if Dustin continues to provoke him. He rummages through his pockets, clearly looking for something.

The party suddenly turns chaotic – people are pushing and shoving, panicking. I freeze for a second, not wanting to believe what I'm seeing. Just moments ago, we were all vibing, and I finally let my guard down, although I had my reservations about coming here from the start. As I try to pull myself together, that little voice in my head chimes in: 'Ebs, you knew things would go left. Why the hell didn't you trust your gut.' I feel angry at myself – my instincts warned me. And now, because I didn't listen to myself, I'm stuck in what feels like a dark, underground dungeon, hoping we all make it out unscathed.

After feeling a surge of nervous energy in my stomach, I force myself not to panic. I carefully scan my surroundings and see Cassius and Aron on my left, looking very serious. I quickly take control of the situation and direct them to exit the venue. It's a trained and instinctive response from growing up in the hood, where we carry a chronic sense of hyper-vigilance, a sixth sense that helps us navigate the inner-city environment. If there is a threat to my safety, I quickly spot the signs. Calculating risk comes with the territory.

The tense and explosive atmosphere in the shubs feels all too familiar to me. I had experienced it so many times before when I heard gunshots, saw flashing lights through my window and cordoned-off crime scenes. In this moment of chaos, my mind plays a video montage of all the tragedies I've witnessed. I can see Bailey's panic-stricken face when he learned that rivals had entered the estate to murder him, the blood gushing from Ash's head when he was gun butted in the face last summer and Cassius's ripped white T-shirt after he had been slashed with a machete. I can't tell you how many vigils I have walked past with lit candles, empty alcohol bottles and balloons in memory of another victim of street violence.

I go back inside, determined to get us all home safely, fully aware of the impending danger and how quickly things can end in yet another tragedy. Scanning the room for Anthony, the lights suddenly turn on, and the music stops. A few women are screaming, and I see the man sitting in a chair surrounded by Anthony and his friends. Each time the man speaks or attempts to get up, he is smacked back down by Anthony's friend, Neville. If this wasn't bad enough, Cassius and Anthony's godbrother, Jamie, steps in, giving him his final warning not to speak or move. Jamie stands behind Cassius, egging him on to spark the man in the face. When I lock eyes with the man, he looks more defeated than threatening.

Cassius is sweating excessively. He's staring at the man intensely. I already knew Cassius could be a hothead, but this is like nothing I've witnessed before. Chin to his chest now, eyes cast down, the man speaks again, this time to Anthony, who looks entirely emotionless, standing there like a soldier ready to go to war. The man's words seem to touch something deep within Anthony, who uses a burst of energy to shout.

'Do you know who I am, my yout?' He pushes his forehead into the man's forehead.

The man is glaring hard at Anthony, who is now rambling. He is trying to assert his manhood and dominance in front of the group. He's what we would describe as 'doing too much'.

I'm charged by what I see, and I'm thinking about the past. Being here is fraught with tension. I speak to them in a way I know the mandem, especially Anthony, will understand, will listen.

'Who are you, Anthony? How can you be asking the man who he is? Who the fuck are you? Just get yourself together, and let's go!' I shout at the top of my lungs, dragging his arm and leading him away from the man. My words silence the entire party. Someone later described my voice as a gun going off.

Anthony stops in his tracks, his eyes wide. He looks at me, clearly embarrassed, and hurries to find the others outside. His friends release the man, and he is encouraged to apologize for disrespecting the mandem. We leave instantly, and as I drive us back to Northville I'm furious the whole way. The mandem sit in the car in complete silence, heads in their hands, embarrassed, just like a couple of schoolchildren being told off by their mother.

We arrive home close to 4 a.m. As I exit the car, I notice the dark sky and no moon in sight. I'm shaking. Until now, I have been running on pure adrenalin, but my body is slowing down from the rush.

My heart beats rapidly, and my thoughts are racing as I let it all out. 'Say someone in the venue decided to jump to the man from South's defence. What would have happened if he was strapped? Say Cassius, with his temperamental self, decided to step to one of the badmen from South,' and I tell them all the ways our night could have easily ended in tragedy had someone made a wrong move. I feel dizzy with the gravity of the situation. A darker energy rises in me, and I grip the railings outside Cassius's house for support.

'What's going on?' Aron asks, as if those are the only words he can manage.

Then Cassius comes out of his house, holding a glass of water. 'It's all right, man. We're safe now.' He tries to comfort me by gently putting his hands on my shoulders and handing me the glass.

Despite their efforts, my tears start to flow.

I weep because I'm a sensitive soul. I weep because I feel drained and confused by what I've just seen. I weep because I'm relieved that no one got hurt. I weep because violence is often the only practical demonstration of manhood in the hood. I weep because violence is celebrated, justified, accepted and tolerated. I weep because the mandem's lives are moulded by a distinct phenomenon: 'acting bad' for status, which compels them to use violence to gain reputation. I weep because this violent phenomenon has wiped out generations upon generations of men in hoods like mine and continues to ravage my community with no end in sight.

I take a sip of water while Cassius stands close, deep in thought. I can see he's struggling to find the right words to comfort me, but the silence between us feels heavy with unspoken emotions. I feel drained and at a loss for words. I mutter a quiet goodbye and head home, seeking the solitude I crave.

The next morning, I wake up surprisingly early at 7 a.m., which is unusual for me. I try to gather my scattered thoughts as each memory rushes through my mind: the serious and angry faces of the mandem, broken glass scattered everywhere, the sounds of shouting, our frantic dash to the car and the tight knot of fear in my throat.

Around noon, I call Cassius to let him know I'm on my way to the Cotch. We need to talk. Despite feeling shocked yet not surprised by witnessing this side of the mandem, I want to understand why 'acting bad' has become a survival mantra in the neighbourhood.

When I arrive at the Cotch, I'm greeted by a scene of happiness. Leanne is outside, watering her cherished crate of white lilies. She's singing along to 'Truth & Rights' by Johnny Osbourne, the steady baseline thumping through the estate.

I head straight up to Aron's room. The moment I walk in, it's giving lazy Sunday vibes. Aron is sitting up in bed, fully in chill mode, hanging with Cassius, Anthony and Ash. The place is a complete mess, almost like a small tornado has torn through it. Clothes are dumped on the sofa, takeaway containers are stacked on the table and dirty cups and plates line the windowsill. It's a bit upsetting to see, but it tells me a lot about Aron's state of mind. The chaos in the room feels like a window into whatever he's dealing with inside. A clear note to self: don't ask him too many deep questions today. Aron is completely absorbed in playing *Call of Duty*, so caught up in the game that he doesn't even notice me enter the room.

Cassius is browsing through his playlist. He selects 'By Your Side' by Tallman and Joe Black and begins enthusiastically reciting the lyrics.

As I climb over the sofa to open the curtains, I can't help but feel frustrated at how different I feel from them. While I'm still trying to process the anxiety from the chaos last night and desperately crave a debrief, they all seem completely at ease, as if nothing unsettling ever happened. I murmur a soft protest, and that's when Aron finally looks up from his game and pays attention.

'C'mon, you're making me lose my flow,' he grumbles, kissing his teeth before immediately returning to his game.

I take a seat on the sofa, feeling a bit uneasy, but I take a deep breath and ask everyone what they thought about what happened yesterday.

Cassius speaks up first, immediately apologizing for losing his temper while I was there. At first, his apology seems genuine, but then he ruins it by calling me a drama queen.

I stare at him, stunned. 'What are you talking about? Are you delusional?' I snap, unable to hide my frustration. 'Yesterday could've ended badly. What if the man from South didn't take the bad up? What then?' Cassius just brushes it off, calling him a fool and insisting he wouldn't have done anything anyway. Anthony leans out of the window, smoking, and quietly nods in agreement.

As Cassius continues to shake his head in irritation, I find myself replaying the events in my mind. All I can remember is how the man from South simply asked Aron why he was leaving, and somehow everything escalated into a contest of who could be the baddest in the room.

Then Cassius has the audacity to laugh at me, saying, 'You

were the one shouting, though,' as if that makes everything okay. I snap back that I wasn't yelling for show – I was actually scared.

Aron hands the PS4 controller to Cassius and turns to me. 'Most of the mandem were pissed cos you were there. That's why they didn't wild out like they wanted to.'

Cassius then casually mentions, 'Anthony even cried in the car after you left.'

I glance at Anthony, who's fuming, trying to deny it. Cassius and Aron exchange amused looks, pretending to wipe away tears. The joke lands, and Anthony shoots them a glare that could kill. But I'm more focused on the truth behind the joke.

'Why were you crying?' I ask him.

Anthony doesn't respond right away. He begins pacing back and forth, mumbling about how the man from South was a pussy who should've known better than to step to Aron. His disgust is clear, but I sense there's more beneath the surface. He's spiralling, and suddenly it hits me – this isn't just about what happened yesterday.

Anthony has always felt the need to prove himself. He's obsessed with how others see him, including me. I used to think his drive for approval stemmed from being older, as if he had to constantly remind everyone he was the real badman. When we were younger, that reputation meant everything to him. People used to say he was a force to be reckoned with, earning his stripes early.

But now I'm starting to realize it's more complicated than just putting on a tough front. What he really craves is respect. Maybe even more than that, he just wants to be acknowledged – even if it means being feared, even if it means leaning into violence. That's the saddest part. He seems to believe that's the only way to earn value in the eyes of others. He thinks if he's not seen as a badman he disappears into the background. Deep down, he might believe that without the badman image he's got nothing left – no pride, no rep, no real sense of self.

'No one can disrespect me,' he finally says, fists clenched at his sides. His voice is low and steady, but I can tell it's barely under control. I try to calm him down, grabbing his arms and looking him straight in the eye, just like I always do when I want him to come back to reality. But this time he pushes me away and storms out of the room.

Once he's gone, the atmosphere feels heavier. The TV is still on, flashing images of *Call of Duty* across the screen, gunfire cutting through the silence. Cassius sits there, staring down at the controller in his lap. Then, suddenly, he bursts out laughing – too loud for the moment. He always does this when things get awkward. It's almost automatic. If he laughs hard enough, maybe he can avoid feeling the weight of the situation, or maybe he hopes we won't notice. Humour is his way of pretending none of it cuts deep. But I know better. We all do.

'Why is everyone moving mad?' Aron asks, clicking off the PS4, which finally goes silent after hours of loud game sounds. He stands up, stretches and rubs the back of his neck, looking more serious as he begins sharing his thoughts.

'It's not that deep,' he says. 'The mandem don't wanna be called a pussy – man will take set on you – and that's why things escalate so fast, because man is always proving that they ain't moist.' The word 'pussy' settles over the room, and

I notice Aron biting his nails, as if struggling to explain something that shouldn't need explaining.

It's clear this word carries more meaning than I initially thought – cutting deeper than a typical insult. I'd heard the mandem throw it around a lot, but now I'm starting to feel how powerful it really is. Being called a pussy feels like wearing a badge of shame, something they fear above all else, and they'll go to extreme lengths to avoid it. Just the idea of being compared to the euphemism of female genitalia makes them see red. On road, that kind of comparison doesn't just offend – it threatens. It paints them as weak, fragile. And in their world there's no space for that, no room for this kind of humiliation. I can see how this pressure affects them; they try hard to avoid even the slightest hint of vulnerability. I noticed this clearly in Anthony's eyes right before he stormed off in anger – he was desperate to maintain his tough image. This constant pressure to never let anyone question their masculinity pushes them to stick to rigid ideas of what it means to be a man: strong, tough and untouchable.

I was starting to realize that the whole badman image comes from this deep fear – the fear of being victimized, ridiculed, called a pussy. To escape that fear, they cling to the image of badness. It's their armour, their shield – a way to hold on to pride in a place that rarely gives them anything else.

'How exactly does one earn badman status?' I ask when Anthony walks back into the room, still sulking, eyes low, his steps heavier than usual. He's holding two black bags, the plastic handles stretched thin by the cans of drinks, a bottle of Lucozade (my favourite) and crumpled packets of crisps. I guess this is his way of apologizing for acting childishly earlier.

The conversation stretches late into the night, and as they talk each explanation pulls me deeper into badman identity. It's complicated, layered. And it means more to them than I first realized.

For some mandem, it starts with getting violated once, then fighting anyone who challenges them, even if it's someone older. Standing up for yourself can get your name known, but it's not just about being violent. It's really about establishing your boundaries and presenting yourself in a way that makes others think twice before disrespecting you.

Just being violent doesn't automatically make you respected. Take Percy, Ash's friend, for instance – he's tough and aggressive, but most people just see him as a joke. Real respect comes from being reliable, standing your ground, backing your boys and showing up when it counts. Sometimes, you don't have to go looking for respect; it comes to you just because you protect those who hesitate.

Cassius shares a unique perspective. He explains that people see him as a badman not just for the bad things he's done, but for the good things too. Being ready to protect family and friends – stepping up when others won't – earns him stripes in a different way.

There's also a sense of resilience and tolerance. Some retreat when crossed; others push all the way, never hesitating when it's time to ride for their people. And the company you keep matters – roll with badmen, and you carry their reputation too.

But, beneath it all, there's a powerful thread running through everything: pride. Cassius picks up on this, diving deeper into what pride means for him.

'It's deep, man, growing up poor in the hood. All you have

is your pride, you know?' he says, through a mouthful of Wotsits. Crumbs fall on to his lap, but he doesn't seem to care. 'Mandem feel powerless in society – you know dem ones. We don't get reputation by going to work, or studying, or them ways. Being a badman on road means something – you are someone.' He tells me he'd rather be bad and respected than a nobody. On road, people rate him. Out there in the wider world, he doesn't get seen at all.

Reflecting on these conversations, I see how deeply toughness and dignity are woven into life in the hood – and I'm not the first to recognize this. Jonathan Ilan captures this dynamic clearly in his 2015 book *Understanding Street Culture: Poverty, Crime, Youth and Cool*.[2] He shows how young men from marginalized urban environments, often excluded from the social and economic mainstream, adopt specific values and behaviours essential for survival. These adaptations shape not only their actions, but also their worldview and sense of identity.

It was becoming clearer to me that being a badman isn't just about status or violence – it's about self-worth. At the core of it is something we all want: to feel seen, to feel like we matter. When traditional pathways to respect and success, like education or employment, feel blocked, this identity becomes a way to gain masculine capital that might otherwise be out of reach. I also noticed that this pride, often tied to a reputation of being 'bad' serves as a strong defence. It shields the mandem from the feelings of shame and insecurity that can come from growing up in disadvantaged urban estates. This identity creates a sense of worth – it's a familiar, achievable form of identity in a world where invisibility often feels like the norm.

I leave the mandem with more questions than answers.

Why is there so little discussion about the role of badman identity – and the dynamics of respect and disrespect – in mainstream conversations about street violence?

Our news is filled with stories about gang violence and crime, painting a bleak image of inner-city life. Government officials and police often double down, introducing harsher tactics like stop-and-search as the go-to solution, yet even after years of implementing these tactics, there's little evidence that they significantly reduce street violence. It seems we might be overlooking something important. In 2024, Keir Starmer's Labour government introduced a £100 million youth programme to cut down knife crime in London, and proposed new laws banning so-called 'zombie knives'. While well-intentioned, these efforts focus more on policing gangs than addressing the deeper causes of street violence.

After speaking with Cassius, Aron, Ash and Anthony tonight, a clearer picture of street violence begins to emerge. Often dismissed as senseless in mainstream discussions, this violence is far more layered. I recognize the logic and structure behind both the violence inflicted and the violence endured. It intertwines with themes of damaged and fragile egos, issues of respect and disrespect and a desperate yearning for pride and self-worth.

It seems to me that the mandem are trying to reclaim identities that have been stigmatized, prove their manhood and establish a viable and respectable reputation on the roads. The prolonged routes to independence for young people in urban areas have led them to adopt a narrow interpretation of 'successful' masculinity. With few resources to achieve the Westernized ideals of masculinity glorified in society, they express their own version of machismo through the badman persona. However, this identity comes with its own limitations. The sociocultural capital it offers is not easily transferable or adaptable beyond the roads. Consequently, adopting this identity often traps the mandem within rigid street codes and behaviours, confining them to their neighbourhood and restricting their potential for upward mobility and broader recognition.

CHAPTER 4

Trap House

On a warm summer night, I find myself standing outside a trap house – a one-bedroom flat tucked away in an ordinary residential building just off Penny Street. It's only a ten-minute walk from the Cotch and not that far from the block. I knew a lot about the trap house through rumours and hearsay before Jacks agreed to take me inside – or so I thought. It had a notorious reputation, and over the years it seemed to attract a lot of trouble and dark scenes, including drug users shooting up outside the property, police raids and attempted robberies. Word on the street is that last week Nelly, a well-known drug dealer, had to chase away a masked man who tried to rob the place. The community's stigmatization of the trap house was understandable, considering the constant trouble it created.

I look up at the dimly lit residential building, thinking Jacks should've been here by now, but there's still no sign of him. The darkness feels dense – as if it's pressing in from all sides. It's the same street I walk during the day, but at night it hits different – it has a whole new eerie vibe. As the minutes drag, every passer-by gets a second glance. I'm alert, unsettled. A sudden rustle from the alley to my left makes my heart jump, but it's just a fox. Then I see a silhouette approaching in the distance. As they get closer, I realize it's Ash.

'What's good?' he asks, looking at me with confusion. 'What are you doing here? Go home, man. You shouldn't be standing out here on your own,' he says as he hurries past me.

He's probably right. I should go home. My watch shows it's 8.30 p.m. Another thirty minutes have passed, and there's still no sign of Jacks. Doubts creep in: has he changed his mind about meeting me at the trap house? After all, it took three long days to persuade him to come here with me. I replay our conversation from last night, his sudden shortness still playing in my mind.

'Jacks, can you take me to the trap house?' I had asked, feeling nervous.

'For what? Why do you need to go there?' he replied, his irritation crackling across the phone like electric static, harsh and uncomfortable.

'I want to understand trapping a bit better,' I explained, trying to keep my curiosity clear. I could almost envision him on the other end rolling his eyes, his frustration mounting as he kissed his teeth.

'I don't want to go in there,' he admitted. His tone revealed his reluctance, even though it was familiar territory for him, almost a second home. We fell into an uncomfortable silence as we processed our unspoken thoughts, until he finally spoke again.

'All right, man, I'll take you. I'll buk you there at around 8 p.m. But I'm not staying there for long. And, Ebs . . . don't ever ask me to take you there again.' His words were short, and he abruptly hung up the phone before I could reply. His tone hit me like a cold splash of water, making me second-guess my decision.

His last words play back in my mind as I wait in the dark,

experiencing the same nervousness I felt when he hung up on me yesterday. Doubts crept in again – was it really wise to ask him to bring me to the trap house? Deep down, I understood that Jacks wasn't eager to let me see the world in which he was involved as a drug dealer.

Since we were teenagers, Jacks has kept the darker parts of his life hidden from me. I caught bits and pieces – fights with boys from rival estates, the time he got arrested for stealing a moped – but, despite our close friendship, he was always good at keeping his struggles locked away. Whenever I tried to bring up certain things, he'd quickly change the subject, leaving me with a bunch of unanswered questions – like trying to solve a puzzle with missing pieces.

As we grew older and took different paths, our bond shifted. He was no longer my go-to, nor was I his, and slowly we drifted apart. Even though we weren't in touch like before, we still found moments to connect, conversing with the same depth we had as teenagers. It was a quiet reminder that, despite the changes in our daily lives, our bond remained strong.

I could still read his emotions like a book. I'd notice how he would tense up or snap if we delved too deeply into his feelings. He often seemed to mentally check out when he felt embarrassed. Last night, I sensed his discomfort on the phone. I could tell that my request to look closer at something he wanted to keep hidden from me made him uncomfortable.

Jacks is a confident person with lots of pride. I had always suspected that he felt ashamed of what he was doing; it's not something of which he was proud, and he worried about my opinion. He didn't want me to think less of him, but I never did. Even though he told himself I was unaware, I always knew about his line of work. Out of love and respect for him,

I chose to honour his need for privacy, realizing how heavy his burden of shame must be.

Jacks never had a job, but had the money to buy luxury cars, go on extravagant holidays and wear designer clothes. His second burner phone was constantly buzzing, and he would sneak away whenever I would go to the block to observe or chat with the mandem. These were the same antics he had displayed in our teenage years. It was clear that he sold drugs to fund his lifestyle, but unlike others who revel in hood fame, he didn't own the label.

I move and sit on the wall outside the building; taking deep breaths and giving myself ten more minutes before I leave. If he stands me up, I reassure myself that I won't be mad. I might call him tomorrow, but I won't grill him, even though he might expect it from me since I used to 'bad him up' when we were younger. My patience and understanding are a testament to our friendship, which has weathered many storms, from dealing with tricky break-ups, to his parents' separation, to all the usual ups and downs of being teenagers. There was even a time when he accused me of not being there for him enough during his break-up with Laura. That led to a few months of silence, but it was always hard to stay angry with him because his sincere apologies would smooth things over and make me forget any hurt feelings.

From the wall on the same side of the street, I have a clear view of the residential building. I absorb the scenery, tracking the movements of the residents who call the flat home. My fascination with people-watching traces back to my childhood, when the world felt like a puzzle waiting to be solved. Many summer holidays after primary school, I would sit at my sister's bedroom window, looking through my binoculars at our neighbourhood, intrigued by what my neighbours were doing. My mind was constantly curious, always wondering who to observe next. Seeing up close through my binoculars, the community never failed to stir something within me. There was something deeply moving about scrutinizing every little detail of people's faces. Each face told a story, and I felt a profound connection. I imagined myself on a personal journey – a quest for understanding and empathy. At eleven years old, I was oblivious to just how captivated I was by the intricacies of human interaction and how people navigated society. My natural curiosity pushed me towards an academic path. Looking back, I realize that becoming a criminologist and ethnographer wasn't accidental – it was a calling that had been whispering to me all along, shaped by what I saw growing up and a deepening interest in understanding what I was seeing.

What one can notice when sitting still and observing without pressure or expectation is truly remarkable. From my vantage point, I see a striking Somali woman in the kitchen on the first floor of the building. She sits with her face in her hands, lost in thought and sadness, tears soaking a pink handkerchief she clutches tightly. Her makeup, untouched by her tears, contrasts sharply with the pain she seems to be feeling. I wonder if she knows I'm watching and why she might be hiding her sadness from her family in the other room. Suddenly, she looks up at a voice calling her, quickly wipes her eyes, and hurries out of sight.

I see a man sleeping in the doorway of the homes opposite me. He has a big pile of empty beer cans nearby. A couple walks by him, but he seems invisible to them, a stark illustration of the social invisibility that often accompanies homelessness. My attention then shifts to a young girl standing at the front entrance of the flat. She is trying to comfort her crying baby while also struggling to get her fussy toddler inside. She shouts at him in a Caribbean accent as he zooms off on his bike, ignoring her calls and adding to her stress. I can't help but chuckle, thinking, *What a little terror!* It makes me realize how tough it can be as a mother with two young kids to take care of.

I switch my gaze to two drug addicts scratching around the wheelie bins a few metres away. They stoop down low, keeping out of view. At this moment, I know they are about to shoot up. I've seen the same scenario play out repeatedly while growing up in the neighbourhood. Observing the raw reality of drug addiction up close and personal doesn't get any easier to digest, though. The thought of what they might be doing makes me uncomfortable. I begin to wonder whether I've made a mistake coming to meet Jacks here. I'm sure I'll witness even more human misery and suffering inside the trap house and question if I can handle it.

As a child, I was deeply saddened by the drug crisis in my community. It unsettled and confused me. As an adult, I now understand that addiction is most prevalent among populations who have endured trauma. Life can be challenging, but life in the neighbourhood is sometimes overwhelmingly distressing. I am witnessing the repercussions of this suffering right in front of me.

After 8:35 p.m., I constantly check my phone, hoping for a message from Jacks. Just as I'm about to give up and leave, I hear the sound of footsteps behind me – getting louder and faster. My heart races, and I turn round abruptly. It's Jacks, his face determined, as if he's on a mission.

'Bloody hell, you scared me, man,' I say, feeling a mix of relief and surprise.

'Relax. What's wrong with you?' he says, his voice calm and soothing. Here I am, on the verge of a panic attack, and there he is, as cool as ever. He pulls me into a tight, comforting hug.

Jacks rummages in his pockets and retrieves a set of keys to let us in. Attached to the gold keyring shaped like a heart is a picture of his daughter, Nia. Seeing it warms my heart – I've always known he had it in him to be a great dad because of his sensitive soul. As he unlocks the door, he steps aside to let two young boys out. They eye us up and down, and one of them says something, but Jacks ignores him. He firmly closes the door behind them as we enter the brightly lit entrance hall.

'Follow me. I want to show you something real quick,' he says, gesturing towards the next set of stairs, which leads up to the roof.

I'm gasping for breath as my lungs work overtime. I wasn't prepared for this sudden bout of exercise, but I don't ask questions. We climb more stairs without exchanging words. I feel a wave of nostalgia as I think back to the times we used to race up to the rooftop of Z Block, the thrill of our footsteps echoing in the empty stairwell, our laughter bouncing off the walls, and the joy of being the first to reach the top. My heart races with that memory. Jacks forcefully opens a heavy door, and we step out on to the flat rooftop.

'The view is a madness from up here, innit?' He smiles as his eyes trace the bright dots in the night sky. The view from the rooftop is stunning. Overhead, countless twinkling stars sparkle like the earring shining in Jacks's ear. It feels as if we are standing at the very edge of the universe, our childhood memories and the present moment blending into one. The stars seem to dance above us, their light painting a breathtaking picture stretching as far as the eye can see, filling us with a sense of wonder.

'It's truly amazing up here.' My voice barely rises above the calming sound of the night. Under the serene night sky, time seems to come to a gentle pause, and our neighbourhood below, lit by the soft moonlight, appears so peaceful and still.

'I knew you would love it up here,' he says, his voice filled with warm memories. 'Do you remember when we used to sit on the roof of the Z Block and just . . . be?' he adds, his gaze fixed on the stars.

We used to sit on the Z Block, even when it was raining or windy, and the raindrops or the howling wind only added to the magic of the moment. There was something about being up there that always seemed to soothe him. It felt like the higher he was, the easier it was to forget about the troubles in his life below. Being up there, above everything else, made his challenges feel smaller, even if just for a little while, and gave him a much-needed sense of peace.

'I suppose you've found another sanctuary,' I say, my head resting on his shoulder. He holds my hand, just as he did when we were teenagers, and I can feel the roughness of his palms against mine, a familiar touch that brings back a flood of memories.

'I wish we could go back to those days,' he reminisces, his voice filled with longing. 'Life was hard back then. I had to step up and be the man of the house, take care of Mum, since my pups pissed off, but, you know, life was simpler back then.'

'What's been happening, Jacks?' I ask.

He shrugs nonchalantly. 'Same old, same old, man. Ain't

got nothing good to share, just the same old shit,' he replies. As he speaks, he points to a shooting star streaking across the sky.

'Make a wish,' he urges, quickly moving the conversation along as the shooting star disappears, leaving a light trail in the dark sky.

'What did you wish for?' I enquire, curious about his secret desires.

'It won't come true if I tell you.' He smiles mischievously.

'You're always full of secrets, aren't you?' I tease, trying to get him to tell me his wish.

'Some things never change, do they?' he says, a flicker of something unreadable in his eyes – like a secret he's not ready to share.

We stand on the rooftop, just like we did as kids, gazing up at the starry night. A cool breeze carries the scent of distant rain, and I sneak a glance at him from the corner of my eye, and memories keep slipping quietly into the present. I can still hear Jacks's voice from those days, pretending to be a scientist, pointing out the stars we used to spot from Z Block. Back then, he was full of dreams for the future. But as we got older the challenges of life started to take their toll on him. I watched from the sidelines as he drifted from one temp job to another – caught deeper in the world of drug dealing and all the politics that came with it. At the same time, he was trying to be a present father to Nia, and taking care of his mum, who had become reliant on a mobility scooter as her health continued to decline.

As we stand in silence, the only sound being the gentle wind rustling around, I am intrigued about what thoughts are running through his mind. Ever since we were kids, he has always been a deep thinker. Now that we're adults, I am not surprised that the mandem call him deep, and Cassius makes fun of him for being too serious. But I know that his cold stare is really just a mask concealing his complex emotions.

Talking to Jacks is always an intellectual adventure. His exceptional ability to pick up on subtle nuances that others miss never fails to impress me. Jacks loves learning and prefers having meaningful conversations over idle chit chat. Unlike some of the group, who seem to be interested in discussing hood politics at length, Jacks possesses a natural curiosity about everything. In another life, Jacks could have easily become the scientist he often joked about.

Jacks is a complex character, and I can see why he might be puzzling to others. One moment, he'll be passionately discussing his favourite subjects, like politics and religion, and the next he seems completely distant, as if he is disconnected from everything and everyone. I've always felt that he's a bit too sensitive for this world. His sensitivity can be a mixed blessing. It sometimes causes misunderstandings and emotional hurt. Having grown up with him, I've noticed his strong moral compass and an ethical backbone, and I know that entering the Trap couldn't have been an easy decision for him. Now, as I plan to ask him about what he does for a living, I'm second guessing my decision, wondering if I really want to hear him explain it to me directly.

The silence between Jacks and me stretches, a few minutes that seem to last an eternity. Finally, he breaks it with an apology.

'Sorry I had you waiting around for me. I was in two minds about coming,' he says, his perfect smile fading into a frown, the lines on his forehead crinkling.

'I felt you had doubts about taking me here. It's cool if you don't want to go in. I could always ask Cassius to be my chaperone for the night,' I say, my laughter tinged with nervousness, trying to lighten the heavy atmosphere.

But Jacks reassures me, his voice low and soothing. 'Nah, it's cool. I'm here now. I'm just warning you: this isn't where I would have wanted to take you. You better let me treat you to lunch tomorrow.' He takes a deep breath, hugging his puffer coat closer to his chest, his eyes darting around as if searching for something or someone.

Despite his reassurance, I can tell he is still apprehensive about taking me inside. The trap house is a place of shadows and secrets. He was nervous about exposing me to the darker aspects of his life – the illegality, the shadow world we used to run from when we were teenagers. I knew he was now fully invested in it as an adult, even though he had vowed never to go near it. He had promised never to live the lifestyle of his cousin Frankie and his uncles.

Growing up, Jacks was always aware of the shadows hanging over his family. His uncles were involved in drug dealing, and Frankie was infamous in our childhood as a notorious drug dealer from Northville, a legacy that Jacks was determined not to inherit. He often spoke about his family's struggles with a mixture of understanding and confusion. He recognized the tough decisions they had to make to survive, but there was always a longing in him for a different life. 'I will never sell drugs,' he would declare, with intense conviction in his eyes. Yet, as the years passed and his own daughter, Nia, became part of the equation, he found himself trapped in a cycle that felt all too familiar, a reality that seemed almost predestined. Now, as we stand together on the roof, I can feel him wrestling with the connection between fate and the choices he made, struggling to find the right words to express how heavy his situation feels.

I say, 'Deal,' as we approach the metal door taking us back downstairs into the trap house. As we walk closer, Jacks begins to fidget and adjust his clothes.

'Are you okay? We don't have to go in if you don't want to,' I say once more, locking my arm into his.

'I'm good. Trust me,' he replies, his eyes fixed on the bright green door in front of us.

He knocks firmly on the door twice, but there is no answer. Before he can try again, I imagine what the atmosphere inside could be. I conjure up a mental image of a sketchy, dirty, abandoned drug den filled with people cooking up crack, like the ones I've seen on popular TV shows such as *The Wire*. Jacks keeps knocking, but there is still no sign of life in the flat.

Just as Jacks is about to give up, a tall, slender, light-skinned man with a spliff hanging from his lips swings the door open, his surprise clear on his face.

'I didn't expect you to show your face again,' he says, eyeing Jacks suspiciously. 'After what your friend did to Trevor, I didn't think you'd be bold enough to come back here.' He stands in the doorway, blocking our entry.

Jacks looks at the man with a cold stare. 'Vic, just cool yourself,' he says, his words laced with a hint of threat. 'Stop your rambling, man.'

As Jacks squeezes past him, Vic tells Jacks about an XL Armani blazer he has for sale for 'a oner'.

'Nah, I'm straight. I don't need any more garms right now,' Jacks says.

'What about you, my love?' Vic turns to me. 'I might have a Prada purse somewhere. Let me go and find it for you.'

'I'm good, Vic. I don't use purses.'

'Come on. You can't still carry your money in your back pocket. You're a woman now. You know that, right?' Jacks teases me.

Vic glances at Jacks and says, 'What a nice girl, Jacks. Too nice for you,' he adds with a wink and asks Jacks for a spliff.

'Nah, it's not like that. Ebs is my longtime friend,' Jacks responds, looking embarrassed.

I take in Vic, his clothing and his behaviour. His crisp, multicoloured suit is neatly ironed, and he has a quick wit.

Vic, also known as Vic Tornado, is squatting in the property. He's renowned for his charming personality, unique fashion sense and quick temper, which earned him his nickname. As far back as I can remember, he has been a well-known thief, stealing high-end designer clothing from luxury stores and reselling them to members of the community, including the mandem, to fund his drug addiction.

Observing the interaction between Vic and Jacks, I see no clear signs of an exploitative or threatening relationship. I don't get the impression that Vic is a victim. In fact, my perception leaned the opposite way – despite Vic being a 'shoot' (a slang term for a drug customer), he appeared comfortable with whatever arrangement is occurring here.

Inside the Trap, the decor is quite different from what I imagined. The walls are covered in shiny wallpaper, and a soft, warm light from the lamps creates a cosy vibe. In the corner, some dishes and cups are waiting to be washed and freshly cleaned clothes rest on the wooden chair by the window. Looking for a place to sit, I observe the glass coffee table, situated in the centre of the room. It is stacked with cannabis bags, digital mini scales and Guinness bottles.

As I clear space on the sofa so that Jacks and I can sit down, Vic settles into a wooden chair by the window, pouring a glass of wine. The calm I feel here is soon shattered by a series of incessant bangs on the front door. Someone outside is shouting and swearing, demanding to be let into the property. Jacks and I exchange worried glances, unsure of what will happen. Vic's eyes widen with fury and determination as I watch him approach the front door.

'Clive, get the hell out of here. How dare you come back here after you and Tina tried to steal from me!'

Jacks's phone rings, interrupting the silence. It's Aron, Cassius and Dee, Ash's godbrother, who are downstairs and now making their way up. Vic is still arguing with the man as Cassius's voice joins them.

'Vic, are you going to let my man take you for a fool?'

The shouting grows louder, mixed with shuffling sounds and a heavy thud. Then, suddenly, the shouting stops as the door swings open and they all flood into the living room. Vic looks different; his composure is gone, and he's dishevelled. They ignore my question about what happened and start arranging themselves in the living room, placing a bucket of KFC on the table.

Vic takes a sip of his wine and sighs. 'That man infuriates me. At least he now knows not to come back around.'

'Where's my duvet?' Dee asks anxiously, his eyes scanning the room.

'Blu, are you still sleeping here?' Jacks asks, his expression one of disbelief.

'Yeah, man, the council won't find me a place, and my mum doesn't want me at home with her new junkie boyfriend,' he explains, grabbing a piece of chicken from the box.

I always make time for Dee, also known as Blu, due to his striking blue eyes. I had met him through Ash and was impressed by his good manners. Although he is only sixteen, he has an old soul. His life is a constant struggle, and he is one of those people who try to see the silver lining in everything, even when life seems to be dealing him one blow after another.

He had been squatting with Vic for six months. It was a temporary refuge for him after being released from the young offenders' institution with no family to turn to. He had been staying with his girlfriend for a while, but her mother recently asked him to leave. During this challenging time, Vic said he could stay on the sofa in exchange for free drugs.

Over the years, I have heard many stories about why the mandem enter the drug economy. However, Dee's situation was particularly troubling. During his early years, he suffered neglect and physical abuse due to his mother's drug addiction and his stepfather's violent tendencies. At age ten, he was placed in care for the first time. Dee managed to complete primary school when his mother was sober, but he was expelled from his secondary school in Year Nine, despite being academically bright and skilled with numbers.

School expulsion is a serious issue that disproportionately affects Black boys, who are overrepresented in exclusion statistics. A recent study in 2024 by the Institute for Public Policy Research and the education charity the Difference[1] highlights that Black Caribbean students continue to experience higher rates of exclusion from schools. Dee's story paints a poignant picture of the dire consequences that arise from inadequate support for vulnerable young people. Instead of receiving the guidance he desperately needed, he was redirected to a Pupil Referral Unit (PRU), which he never attended due to the difficulties he faced at home.

This lack of access to structured support has left Dee feeling adrift, lost and directionless, with essential safety nets that could have paved the way for a brighter future completely absent. Caught in what I can only term the 'school-to-trap-life' pipeline, Dee is stuck in a devastating cycle. Many young people like him struggle to acquire crucial social skills, education and job training, rendering them ill-equipped to thrive within mainstream society. This sense of exclusion from normal societal structures often pushes them towards the drug trade in a desperate attempt to escape their marginalized status within an inequitable social hierarchy that continually relegates them to the bottom of the structural food chain. To make matters worse, Dee also faces the added challenge of not having a safe place to rest, further entrenching him in a precarious situation that seems devoid of hope and opportunity.

As Dee digs into his chicken, I sit beside him, quietly, watching him eat as if he hasn't had a meal in ages. It's been months since we last saw each other, but I still recall how his voice trembled the last time we talked. He sounded so lost, as if he was clinging to tiny bits of hope just to keep himself together.

'Hey, Dee, it's been a while. How've you been?'

His eyes stay fixed on the box of hot wings. For a moment, I wonder if he's going to respond at all. Then a long, tired sigh escapes him – deep, as if he's been holding it in for days.

'Life's just . . . hard,' he mutters. 'It's always me. Bad things just keep happening.'

His voice isn't angry — it just sounds worn out, as if he's not even surprised any more. I can see it in his face: the frustration, the heaviness, the kind of exhaustion that sleep doesn't fix.

I'm not sure what to say — words feel too light for the weight he's carrying. So I reach out and take his hand, gently, worried he'll pull away. His fingers are cold. He doesn't look at me, but he doesn't let go either. Sometimes, you don't need words. Just being there, really being there, is enough to remind someone they're not alone.

Dee finishes off his chicken, licking the grease from his fingers one by one, taking his time and making a lot of noise. The sound fills the room, and I notice Cassius side-eyeing him. You can almost feel his patience wearing thin.

'Fix up, man. Why you looking for sympathy?' Cassius snaps, his tone sharp but not completely unkind. 'You just need to trap harder, my G. No one's coming to rescue you.'

'I am trapping hard, twenty-four–seven, man,' Dee fires back, his voice shaky with a mix of pride and desperation. 'I'm grinding to make it.'

Cassius crosses his arms and leans back, clearly unimpressed. 'You're not making no money, my brudda. If you was, you wouldn't be in this situation, would you? You're not living the dream, camped out on Vic's sofa.'

The words hit hard. Dee looks down at the floor, but he doesn't back down. 'It's different for you, blud. You've been trapping for time — I just jumped on this ting,' he says, locking eyes with Cassius. It surprises me — no one ever has chat for Cassius, except Aron.

'Just watch, by the time I'm your age,' Dee continues, 'I'll have my own yard, a car. Man will be flossing, and man will respect me.' There's determination in his voice, even if it feels fragile, trying to grow in a space that keeps pushing it down.

Cassius just shakes his head, but, surprisingly, he doesn't cuss him. 'Well, you better fix up real quick then and stack your Ps, so you can pattern your life.' His tone makes it clear: end of discussion.

Dee doesn't argue; he just leaves the room, his silence louder than any reply.

Aron calls out to him and then turns to Cassius, voice calm and steady. 'Allow him, man. It's hard out here – you should know that better than anyone. Everyone wants to make it, yeah? But the trap is brutal. If you ain't smart with your money and get caught up in the glitz and all that fake shit, you burn through it fast. My man is just trying to survive. He can't think about saving for the future when he's living hand to mouth.'

Cassius sighs, scratching his head. 'Yeah, I hear you . . . But, you know, there are levels to this. He's just on some low-level shit and ain't even making no real P.'

As I listen to the tense back-and-forth between Cassius and Aron, I start to think about what 'making it' really means to them. Success in the drug trade seems tied up with financial independence, stability and respect on the roads. Just like capitalism pushes consumerism, greed and cash over moral values, the mandem hold on to those same conservative ideals – they want all the things society says are valuable. They chase materialism, status and independence – expectations that feel normal in a modern world driven by acquisitive individualism. For them, the drug trade offers a faint glimmer of hope – a chance to better their lives that feels just out of reach in mainstream society. It's a small opportunity they seize because the usual routes to success don't seem open to them.

I'm sitting here with a flood of questions, especially about what Cassius said – this idea of 'different levels to this'. It's a quiet admission that trapping isn't some one-size-fits-all hustle; it's layered, complex, with different shades and tiers. That thought takes me back to a conversation I had with him, Aron, Ash and Anthony just weeks before I visited the trap house. They laid out the different ways the mandem earn a living in the drug economy. I turn to Aron and ask if he can break it down again – explain what those levels really mean.

He blinks slowly, as if he's flipping through pages in his mind. Then he leans in and says:

'Like I was telling you the other day. There are different mandem and different levels of desperation. Man have different morals. We ain't all the same; we are doing it for different reasons. Some man are sleeping on next man's floor. Someone like that is gonna trap hard – he will rob women or do some other fuckery; he's greedy. Then you have man that have heard their mother on the phone crying because next man has kicked off her door because of some fuckery that he did – robbing next man. He is on road, angry, willing to kill, do whatever. Some man are humble, just wanna make money and keep a low profile. Some humble man even have a job – you have some man that work and still trap.'

Whenever we discussed the drug economy, the term 'trapper' came up often. Listening to Aron break it down this evening, it becomes even clearer that trappers are not a monolith; they fall into distinct categories. With insights from Aron and the other mandem, I developed a trapper typology to make sense of these layers – grouping trappers into three main types: the glutton trapper, driven by an insatiable hunger for money and street validation; the predatory trapper, who survives by robbing or exploiting others in the game; and the humble trapper, who moves through the drug economy quietly, often reluctantly, with hopes of eventually leaving it behind. As part of my academic work,[2] I formalized this typology to help explain how trappers adapt their strategies depending on their circumstances, opportunities, needs and the psychosocial trauma they carry.

Dee, now back and having missed our earlier conversations about different types of trappers, leans in, clearly interested in what Aron's been saying. He tilts his head and lets out a small laugh, which is the first hint of humour I've seen from him all evening. 'So, what type of trapper am I, then?'

I pause, studying him. Already, I can see the profile forming – he fits the glutton trapper. Shaped by deep-rooted trauma and an upbringing marked by extreme poverty, glutton trappers often move through the world with a potent mix of desperation and hunger for money. Their experiences tend to push them into what Malcolm Klein[3] once described as cafeteria-style offending – a term referring to wide-ranging involvement in different types of crime, rather than sticking to one.

'I think you fit the glutton trapper profile,' I respond, explaining my reasons carefully. I know Dee can be unpredictable – he's not just a typical drug dealer. He moves between selling drugs and committing street robberies, changing his approach based on what he needs at the moment or what's happening around him.

He shifts in his seat, his expression serious yet soft. 'Is that really how you see me?' His voice is quiet. Not defensive – just curious. He pauses to light a cigarette. 'Yeah . . . I guess I am hungry for money, cos man is a proper sufferer,' he admits, then adds, voice steady but raw: 'Yeah, I rob people . . . I don't really care who I rob – I just need the money.' I notice his chest rise and fall, and then I see his swollen lip. It's a visible reminder of the price he's already paid – and maybe of what's still to come.

'What happened to your lip, Dee?' I ask gently. He rolls his eyes and shakes his head, a bit annoyed by my question. Eventually, he lets it slip that he had been punched in the face by someone he robbed. He needed quick cash because he hadn't eaten in days.

As Dee continues sharing his thoughts, there's another abrupt knock at the door that cuts him off. The constant flow of people passing through makes the place feel like Clapham Junction station.

Jacks, who'd been quiet up until now, finally speaks, irritation creeping into his voice.

'Why don't you just sell a little herb?' he asks. 'You're not making any money doing what you're doing, and people don't respect man who violate others. You're acting way too desperate.'

Dee shakes his head, trying to defend himself. He explains to Jacks that he's already tried selling weed, but it didn't bring in any real P.

Without another word, Jacks abruptly stands up, his chair scraping loudly against the floor. 'I'm going to the toilet,' he mutters, already tuning out of the conversation.

Dee just sits there, confused and slightly embarrassed, still half talking to himself. Then he turns to me, almost pleading.

'I know some mandem think I'm a wasteman because of how I make my P.'

Before he can finish, Cassius cuts in with a sharp edge: 'Glad you know that. Mandem who are prepared to sell their souls on the roads can't be trusted. Didn't you rob your boy the other day?'

Dee cuts his eye, telling him to 'shut up', clearly not wanting that to come out. His frustration builds, and he turns to the rest of the room, insisting that he isn't a liability – that he deserves to be put on, that he needs to make money.

He and Cassius go back and forth. Dee tries to prove he's a badman, while Cassius shakes his head, calling him 'moist', reminding him that no one's asking about badness – that he's always trying to prove himself.

From the corner of my eye, I see Aron shift, clearly irritated. He finally steps in, telling Cassius to ease up on Dee.

I'm grateful for the intervention. I've always felt Dee needed a little extra kindness. He's only sixteen, and his life is already spiralling out of control. He moves through a world full of risk and violence, made worse by childhood trauma and the relentless pressures on road to earn 'street capital'. Because he lacks the social status of trappers with higher social standing, he is more vulnerable to serious harm. It's sad that, to counter this, he needs to respond with indiscriminate violence just to survive.

As I sit in contemplative silence, absorbing Dee's raw experiences, it becomes clear – as I've argued in my academic work – that both conscious and unconscious forces influence his choices and behaviour. Psychosocial criminologists Gadd and Jefferson shed light on how people respond to crisis and trauma, showing that a complex interplay of conscious and unconscious motivations often shapes crime and violence. On the surface, Dee appears to engage in drug dealing and minor street crimes as a means of survival. But beneath this straightforward facade lies a deeper emotional undercurrent. I sense hidden influences – unresolved trauma and deep-seated emotional conflicts – silently guiding his decisions.

As I delve deeper into Dee's criminal activities and the ways glutton trappers like him earn illicit gains, a clearer picture begins to emerge; his choices seem heavily fuelled by a profound contempt for the poverty he endured during his formative years. Memories of powerlessness and deprivation weigh on him, pushing him to take his stress out on the roads by acting out core wounds – feelings of being unwanted, weak and helpless.

These emotional scars are made worse by Dee's low status in the world of trapping, where his way of earning money isn't respected by other trappers. Dominated and devastated by the loss of approval and love from his primary caregivers and peers, Dee appears to be on a desperate quest to feel valued, seen and affirmed. This relentless search creates a troubling mix of ambition and despair, echoing Sigmund Freud's concept of 'repetitive compulsion'[4] in which Dee is trapped in a cycle of re-enacting early traumas, caught in an anxious struggle to rescue his identity from stigma, to redeem himself, to prove his credibility on road and finally to earn the love and respect he was denied. The harsh truth is that no matter how much money Dee accumulates, no matter how many people he cheats, or how many friends he betrays in his pursuit of wealth, his circumstances remain unchanged. His past traumas continue to torment him, and the way he makes his income only intensifies his suffering.

There is another knock at the door, and Vic goes to answer it. I can hear him mumble to the person outside. Jacks is tired, and I know he wants to leave, but before he can say it Smithy enters the living room. Smithy is known for preying on and robbing drug dealers. As soon as he walks in, the mood changes quickly from light to heavy.

Smithy greets everyone with a smirk on his face, saying, 'Yo, my youts, what's with the silence?' I notice that everyone except Aron looks uncomfortable. Smithy's reputation precedes him, and the way in which he makes money in the Trap adds to the tension.

'You good? What are you doing here?' Smithy asks me, his voice calm but unreadable.

He's tall and imposing, infamous for his trademark black shades that conceal his eyes. The mandem told me he wears them year-round so no one can see who he's watching, or who he's planning to move on next.

I greet him hesitantly. He now prefers to be called Champs – short for Champion – but I haven't quite adjusted to the change yet. Thankfully, he lets it slide, walking into the room with quiet authority.

He shrugs off his long black parka and slides off his Prada beanie, revealing a fresh trim underneath. Then, with effortless confidence, he drops into the sofa, positioning himself directly between me and Dee. The shift in the room is immediate. Dee stands up without a word and quietly moves to the far side, putting distance between them.

I've known Smithy for many years, long before he became a well-known trapper. Now in his early thirties, he has transformed from the quiet and timid boy I once knew on our estate. Back then, he wasn't interested in the limelight, even though girls flocked to him, drawn to his chiselled features and muscular build. He didn't enjoy the attention. Now, he's a different person, confident and self-assured, using his looks to his advantage. He licks his lips, a subtle gesture that hints at his arrogance. Smithy likes to present himself as the strong, mysterious, silent type and doesn't usually initiate conversation, but tonight he's up for talking. He removes his sunglasses, revealing his swollen eyes, as though he has been up all night. When I ask about his motivations for drug dealing, he holds my gaze and takes control of the conversation.

'I'm not into low-level drug dealing, I'll leave that for the youts. I've been there and done that. Can't make no money selling drugs on the block. I don't see the sense in selling crack. That's just like a normal nine-to-five: doesn't make you real money, and you're still gonna suffer. You know how much man I know who trap, but don't have anything to show for it? Standing on the block, trapping to crackheads, robbing people on the street, some low-level shit and they ain't even getting paid.'

Smithy holds himself in higher regard than the average trapper grinding on street corners. That kind of hustle, in his eyes, is beneath him. He specializes in high-risk, high-reward deals – the kind that demand less graft and promise bigger pay-offs.

He's driven by ego and image. You'll see him cruising around Northville in an expensive car, kitted out in designer gear and diamond jewellery. Maintaining that look isn't just a side effect of his lifestyle – it's the whole point.

When I ask about how he justifies the risks, he doesn't

hesitate. His voice carries a hint of superiority as he says, 'To put it simply, I'm not like the other mandem. If I'm going to take on the risks on road, I'm going to make sure I get paid. Let me be clear. Yeah, me and my mandem rob drug dealers – but only drug dealers with proper P.'

He says it like it's the most logical thing in the world, his tone cool and matter of fact, despite the weight of what he's admitting.

Smithy is the archetype of a predatory trapper, a name given to men on road who prey on and target other trappers in pursuit of their ill-gotten gains. These men are overly ambitious in their pursuit of money, success and prestige, and their ambition is to steal from and rob others involved in the illegal economy. They never target anyone outside this group.

Smithy reminds me a lot of Omar Little from *The Wire*[5] – an iconic character who famously said, 'A man gotta have a code.' Omar shows that even people outside the law can live by their own sense of right and wrong. Smithy is much the same. He might reject society's rules, but he follows his own strict principles. As a ruthless predator who targets only fellow trappers, Smithy personal moral code clearly sets the limits of his criminality. That's what sets him apart in a world full of moral ambiguity. Unlike glutton trappers, like Dee, who prey on innocent and vulnerable people through street robberies, Smithy consciously avoids crossing that line. His code determines who he targets in the drug trade, and the substantial profits he earns give him significant status among his peers, distinguishing him from others still struggling to survive.

As I listen to Smithy's animated descriptions about making money in the drug economy, I'm curious to know what the others in our group think of his methods, but I can feel the atmosphere tighten whenever Smithy talks, and I decide against asking. Of everyone, Cassius is the one most uncomfortable with Smithy in the room. Smithy's associates robbed his uncle once, and as a result Cassius isn't his biggest fan. The tension among them reveals to me the murky dynamics of the illegal economy.

'I'm gone, you know,' Cassius says to Aron, giving Smithy an evil glare as he leaves.

I'm relieved Cassius chose to go rather than get involved in his uncle's beef. He is not foolish; he knows Smithy's credibility and well-established position in the Trap. Men like Smithy are the untouchable elite of the road-culture milieu and reign supreme in their sector, because they are both respected and feared. Youngers like Cassius, who are wise to the game, understand the dire consequences of crossing their path.

It's just after 11 p.m., and the mood is lively as everyone drinks, chats and smokes. I stay close to Smithy, trying to figure out the layers of his mind and his life. We explore uncharted territory by discussing his childhood, family and life experiences. It is a revelation to see Smithy open up. I start to piece together a picture of his conscious and unconscious motivations for his work. While the allure of making money by targeting those who already have drug wealth may seem like a straightforward incentive, I am starting to realize that there is a deeper and more intricate story.

Smithy scrolls through the photos on his phone, proudly sharing pictures of his three children. Then he suddenly stops at a photo of himself as a teenager – just a fifteen-year-old boy. In the picture, he's wearing a dirty white vest, ripped shorts and trainers without laces. He looks up at me, clearly uncomfortable, his eyebrows scrunched together, and says, 'Can you believe that was me?'

I quickly tell him he was handsome back then, but he brushes it off coldly: 'That yout was poor – fuck being handsome!'

The photo stands in stark contrast to the successful man he's become. It feels like a missing puzzle piece in his journey into the Trap, something that intrigues me – maybe a reminder of the struggles he had to overcome. I wonder if that moment influenced his future path.

Leaning back on the worn sofa, Smithy continues to share his story, disdain tugging at the corners of his mouth. He recalls how the mandem used to laugh at him – mocking his worn-out trainers that seemed to 'talk' and his dutty clothes. He speaks quietly about the vivid dreams that kept him going back then: fantasies of owning his own place, stacking Rolexes on his wrist, and dressing in clothes that marked success rather than struggle. A deep, genuine laugh escapes him, a mixture of disbelief and pride. Now, he says, no one is laughing any more – he's living the dream most mandem only ever imagine. There's a sparkle in his eyes as he talks about how he's 'always looking fresh to death, all day, every day.'

During our long conversation, which lasts over an hour, Smithy shares more of his journey to where he is today. He reveals even more moments that left him feeling ashamed – begging for food, feeling embarrassed by his mother's lifestyle and being teased because of his appearance. These experiences have clearly left a lasting mark, and I sense unresolved toxic shame driving his commitment to robbing others and chasing a luxurious lifestyle, so far removed from his difficult home life.

Stories like Smithy's – typical of the predatory trapper – aren't just about poverty or crime. They reveal how poverty can embed itself deeply in a person's psyche. Compelled by survival and a desperate need to reclaim self-respect and autonomy, these men have honed their skills as prolific robbers.

Shame is a universal human experience that everyone faces at various points in their lives. It often feels like a heavy sense of not being good enough, as if we're flawed or lacking in some way when we think about how others see us. This complicated feeling affects how we view ourselves and can impact the way we interact with the people around us.

Psychiatrist James Gilligan[6] talks about how feelings of shame can lead to behaviours like crime and violence. When I listen to Smithy explain why he chose his line of work, I can sense he is carrying a lot of emotional baggage. Deep down, it feels as if he is trying to protect that vulnerable kid he used to be – the one who grew up in poverty and felt as if he had no control over his life – behind a facade of success. Smithy has reinvented himself, with an identity that earns him recognition as a 'money man' in Northville.

This reminds me of the idea of the 'false self', introduced by British psychoanalyst Donald Winnicott.[7] In the 1960s, he described this concept to explain how people create a mask to protect their real, vulnerable selves from emotional hurt and unmet needs. Like many other predatory trappers I've met, Smithy often seems to crave attention and shows signs of narcissism. He flaunts his wealth, showcasing the luxuries that come with his lifestyle. But it isn't just about bragging; it is a strategic effort to gain 'hood fame', respect and status among the mandem. At the same time, this behaviour – the mask he wears – helps him hide the deeper feelings of worthlessness and powerlessness he experiences outside the hood in wider, mainstream society.

But like Dee, and many others shaped by childhood poverty, Smithy is emotionally fragile and seeks constant validation and admiration. His early experiences have led him to believe that violence is not only acceptable, but necessary – a justified way to acquire material wealth and to maintain his reputation. Over time, this belief has hardened into a self-protective narrative.

After midnight, Jacks glances at the clock and starts to yawn. 'You done quizzing everyone?' he asks me, half smiling.

Smithy jumps in, laughing, saying I've picked his brain enough for one night. He playfully calls me 'the little therapist', joking that he's shared too much already – but beneath the laughter I can tell he means it.

After Jacks taps my knee for the third time, I take the hint and stand up, thanking everyone for their time. The moment I say my goodbyes, I notice the change – the mood shifts back to business. Smithy's voice changes too, slipping back into his usual controlled, authoritative tone as he starts talking to Vic. It's like a scene change in a play, the atmosphere snapping back to formality.

I ask Jacks if he's heading straight home, and he says no, then offers to walk me to my car. Outside, it's quiet and calm, and Jacks is unusually silent. The streetlights flicker above us, casting our long shadows on the pavement, creating an almost ghostly feeling, as if another presence is walking with us.

He seems tense, but I can't hold back any longer. 'Why haven't you ever told me what you do for work?'

Before he can respond, Cassius zooms past in his car, and

for a moment everything feels suspended in the glare of headlights and the sound of the engine. Jacks pretends he didn't hear me, but I'm not letting it go this time.

I stop walking and turn to him. 'Why can't you just tell me?'

He hesitates, and there's a long pause before he softly replies. 'I'm not like you. I'm not where I need to be in life right now.'

His words hit hard because I know he means them, and I feel the familiar ache of watching someone I care about struggle.

'Is that how you see it, Jacks? That I'm exactly where I need to be?' I ask. 'Because I'm not. I still feel lost sometimes.'

I look at him, hoping my honesty might help him open up. 'I'm still trying to work it all out! This research, it's the only thing keeping me focused. It gives me direction, some kind of meaning.'

Jacks looks at me with the same quiet curiosity he always has, but he doesn't respond — he just stares at me as we approach the car. So I try again, gently, hoping to break through his walls.

'You know I'd never judge you, right? I just want you to be happy. Are you?'

'What's the definition of happiness?' he asks, half smirking in that way he does when he's about to get philosophical.

I don't answer. I don't know how to.

'If we're going by the standard definition,' he continues, 'then no. I ain't content. I don't really feel joy . . . only a little, I guess, when I'm with Nia. When I'm with her, her laughter and her presence bring me a little happiness. But it's not enough to fill the void.'

His voice trembles slightly, and I hear it – the weight of that emptiness he rarely lets anyone see.

I look down, unsure of what to say. 'What happened, Jacks? You had all these hopes and dreams when we were kids.'

'Life happened,' he says. 'I got stuck. I got trapped.'

I wait, giving him space. Then he speaks. 'You know what I do. Stop playing. You're the smartest girl I know. I can't keep secrets from you, even if I want to. You always figure it out.'

He tries to laugh, but there's a heaviness in his voice that betrays him. The shame, the tiredness, the quiet resignation of someone who's been surviving for too long are all felt in the silence between us. And then, after a deep exhale, he blurts it all out.

'I'm stuck in the same trap as everyone else, struggling to survive,' he says. 'I'm not taking the same risks as some of the other mandem. I keep a low profile, stay humble, just doing my ting, selling a little green here and there.'

He shakes his head, nearly banging it against the car door as he gets in. 'I used to be properly in the trap, but man grew up and realized I can't trap forever. The thing is, I don't have an exit plan. You know I didn't finish school, didn't go college or uni. I've worked a few driving jobs here and there. I do dip in and out of mainstream. I'm working at some warehouse at night, but it's hard out here.'

He exhales, voice flat now. 'I'm not making any money the legit way. I can't take care of Nia or myself on minimum wage – you get me. So I have to trap until I figure it out.'

At this moment, when Jacks reveals his drug dealing to me for the first time, part of me wishes I'd remained ignorant — because now I feel his struggle more than ever. I'd had my suspicions that he was selling drugs to make ends meet, but hearing him say it out loud makes one thing clear: he isn't doing it for clout or status. He isn't flashy. He isn't trying to build a name for himself. He just wants to survive.

The way he speaks, the choices he makes, show me that Jacks is a humble trapper, one of the most common types of drug dealers on road. Unlike predatory trappers, who often work in groups and chase reputations, humble trappers tend to operate alone. They move quietly, often with one foot in the legal economy, using drug dealing to supplement the low pay of insecure, minimum-wage jobs. They're hoping to leave the trade behind one day. For many, it's a means to an end — not a career, but a survival strategy. So they deal what sells: cannabis, ecstasy, heroin, cocaine — and they keep their heads down, doing what they call 'the hard work' in the overall division of labour.

Jacks and I sit in the car for hours as he opens up about his life and what he does for a living, filling in all the gaps I'd misunderstood. He tells me his mum struggled with depression, and things got even worse after his dad left. Some days, it was so bad she couldn't even get out of bed. From a young age, Jacks had to take on everything — looking after the house, getting his little sister ready for school, cooking meals (which he jokes were mostly cheap frozen food), and managing the bills when the income support came through. Even when he wanted to break down from the pressure, he felt like he couldn't — his mum and sister needed him too much. As Jacks shares his story, I feel a heaviness in my chest. I'd had no idea how tough things had been for him at home. It makes me think about how he's always been everyone else's emotional support – but who was there for Jacks when he needed help?

Jacks, like many of the humble trappers I've encountered, found himself pulled into the drug economy – driven by a complex mix of pressures, with financial instability at the centre. But there was something different about his background compared to others. While they all experienced childhood poverty, Jacks's upbringing was less marked by violence, severe neglect or abandonment. His mother's depression shaped his early years, but he wasn't exposed to the same extreme conditions others had faced.

As uncomfortable as it is to see Jacks this vulnerable, his honesty helps me understand why he leaned on the trap's false promise of a better life. He believes he can find some kind of stability through dealing – maybe even reach the level of success Smithy has. But the more I listen the more I realize – and I think he does too – that the life he is chasing always seems just out of reach.

He understands that the Trap isn't a real solution. It doesn't bring peace or freedom. It only deepens the wounds he already carries. The violence – the uncertainty, the shady dealings – they add new layers of trauma, stacking on top of the pain he never got to process from childhood.

'I wish I never even started trapping,' Jacks confesses, slipping off his Jordan trainers – seeking comfort in a familiar space. His words linger, filled with regret and a sense of lost potential.

'The Trap changed me, man,' he says, gazing out of the window as if he's searching for clarity in the chaos around him.

I look at him, stunned by the admission. 'You're still the

same old Jacks to me,' I say, hoping to reassure him – hoping it's still true.

'I'll always be the same Jacks to you, Ebs,' he replies softly. 'But I can feel myself getting more ruthless.'

His honesty sends a chill through me. This isn't bravado; it feels like a warning.

'What are you talking about, Jacks? Your heart's too pure to ever become ruthless,' I say, trying to keep fear out of my voice. But the thought of him slipping into darkness is hard to bear.

'I just wanted to make a little extra P, but the trap don't work like that. It's sucked me in,' he says, shaking his head. 'Man robbed my tings the other day . . . and I can't let that slide.'

It's his certainty that scares me the most. It's not anger – it's determination.

'I'm in deep now. They've drawn me out.'

I understand exactly what he means. I've seen it happen – how the roads slowly consume the mandem, even the kindest souls. The longer they stay involved, the more they change, becoming shadows of their former selves. To survive the violence, they often end up caught in it.

'When I think I'm getting out, some madness always happens to pull me back in,' he says. 'It's fucked. Got me questioning myself . . . making me think dark thoughts about what I'd do to them.'

His voice doesn't rise – it sinks, heavy with exhaustion. I can feel the war inside him: his values versus the anger that the trap brings out in him. The need to protect himself against the fear of being seen as weak. It's a quiet torment, but relentless.

'Jacks, you need to get away,' I tell him. 'Just leave the estate for good.'

'I know. I'm trying, man. I will get out eventually, I promise,' he says – but the promise sounds empty, as if it's already slipping away.

As I leave Jacks just after 2 a.m., I watch him walk away – shoulders hunched, head down. I drive off knowing the painful truth: Jacks is trapped between two worlds, and neither brings him peace. He felt heavier tonight, as if life was pressing down harder than usual.

He longs for a better life – one filled with hope and security. But the trap keeps pulling him back with its promises of quick P, a taste of power and elevated status. The roads have turned into more than just a hustle; it's become a fierce battleground, testing the very essence of who he is. And Jacks is caught in the middle, struggling to stay true to himself as violence inevitably comes knocking on his door and he's forced to settle old scores.

This is a familiar story among many trappers involved in drug dealing. They often live with fear, stress, paranoia and constant hypervigilance. Over time, they realize that the drug economy is a dead end – offering little opportunity and a life filled with treacherous unpredictability. Though initially drawn by its perceived benefits, the harsh reality of violent victimization soon shatters this illusion. By the time they awaken to this truth, often as they get older, they feel trapped in their lifestyle, and the idea of escape seems almost impossible.

For a long time, I thought the drug economy mostly caught men trying to escape poverty and make quick money.

But the deeper I looked, the more I realized it's much more complicated than that. It's tied to a wider psychosocial crisis – lack of education, long-term unemployment, street pressure and both past and ongoing trauma. All these factors make people vulnerable, pulling them into the drug trade. At its core, it's about being disconnected from mainstream society, from opportunity, from hope. The dream of a better life draws the mandem in, and even when they know the risks, they still step into it. For many, dealing drugs isn't just a choice – it's a means of survival and a way to gain some footing in a world that often feels unforgiving.

CHAPTER 5

Mosque

It's been almost a month since I last spoke to Jacks at the trap house. After that emotional night in my car when he shared his feelings, I tried to call him a few times, but he didn't respond. Last week, after my third attempt, he finally sent a message that read, 'I'll call you in ten minutes,' along with a thumbs-up emoji. This vague reassurance is classic Jacks; it's his way of reaching out when he feels overwhelmed. After receiving this message, I gave him the space he seemed to need.

I'm about to have a shower when my phone vibrates on the counter. Quickly, I dry off my hand and reach for it, trying to answer before it stops. I miss the call, but my phone is vibrating with messages and the phone keeps on ringing.

'Where are you?' It's Nathaniel, Jacks's cousin, on the other end, his voice filled with a sense of urgency. 'Did you hear about what happened to Jacks last night?'

My heart quickens its pace, and my entire body tenses in anticipation. Taking a deep breath, I murmur, 'Is he hurt?'

The call is particularly alarming as Nathaniel has deliberately distanced himself from the mandem and the roads to focus on his 'Deen', a term, rooted in Arabic, that denotes the complete Islamic way of life guiding one's existence. In UK street slang, living a righteous Muslim life is often described as being 'on (my) Deen'. Nathaniel rarely contacted the mandem these days, so his return to Northville clearly indicated the seriousness of the situation and his deep concern about Jacks. It stirred a sense of unease within me.

Nathaniel recounted the harrowing events from the previous night. Jacks and Neil, his best friend, had returned from a nine-night and were sitting in their car outside Neil's house unaware of any incoming danger. As they got ready to exit the car, an unfamiliar vehicle approached, carrying several individuals they didn't recognize. A young boy stepped out and asked where Neil and Jacks were from. When he received no response, he drew a knife. Moments later, others jumped out of the vehicle and surrounded Neil's car, tapping their weapons against the windows. Sensing the danger, Jacks and Neil decided to leave the car and run. As they fled, Jacks was struck on the head, but they managed to escape to safety.

'Come to the mosque. Jacks is outside, just staring into space; he's not himself. He hasn't slept, and he's still in the same clothes from last night.' He ends the call soon after.

I have never been to a mosque before, but I understand the connection the mandem have to it through heartfelt conversations I've had with them. They speak of Islam enthusiastically, describing it as a truthful and beautiful religion that brings them comfort and clarity amid the challenges on road.[1] From our conversations, I sense that the mosque exudes an atmosphere of deep reverence and profound spiritual transformation, serving as a sacred sanctuary for many former trappers, like Nathaniel, who bravely decided to leave their lives of crime and violence behind.

I quickly get ready to leave, my heart racing with anticipation at the thought of finally seeing Jacks and hoping he's okay. I make my way to the mosque located at the edge of the estate. I try to call him several times, but he doesn't pick up. As I get closer to the mosque, I notice Nathaniel outside, engaged in a lively conversation with a group of young boys. Despite looking around eagerly, I can't see Jacks anywhere.

Approaching Nathaniel, I immediately notice his appearance has changed. He wears a long, flowing white Islamic thobe, a vibrant red-and-white kufiya and Islamic prayer beads round his neck. His once clean-shaven face is gone: he has grown a carefully groomed beard. This is a departure from the Nathaniel I remembered, who was always impeccably dressed in expensive designer clothes and sported a sharp fade haircut every week without fail.

When I join the group, Nathaniel greets me with the traditional Muslim salutation '*As-salaam alaikum*', and a warm and welcoming smile. He continues his conversation with the young boys, reciting verses from the Holy Quran. Each verse holds a mesmerizing power that captivates all of us. We're enthralled by the depth of his recitation, and it feels as though we are witnessing a newfound sense of peace radiating from Nathanial. His enthusiasm and passion for his new philosophy on life are palpable. He shares with the youngsters how Islam has transformed his life, illuminating a different path for him. He speaks about the profound contentment that comes from forming a close relationship with God and how happy he is to adhere to the teachings of the Quran.

Back in the day, Nathaniel was a young boy of few words; his speech was often tinged with violence, and his mind was preoccupied with get-rich-quick schemes. He had fully embraced a life on road, and by the age of twenty-four he had earned notoriety as a predatory trapper. His life was a constant battle with stress and anxiety. But now he stands before me a transformed young man.

His once troubled demeanour now radiates with hope and positivity. His past, once a haunting memory, is now a distant echo. His words carry a different weight, his actions a different purpose. His transformation is nothing short of inspiring.

He notices me. 'You just missed him. I was supposed to call you and let you know that he left, but, you know, I had to impart some knowledge to the younger ones and got sidetracked. My bad,' Nathaniel says with pride in his voice.

'Don't worry, Nathaniel. Listening to you speak so passionately about Islam made me forget why I came to meet you,' I respond, smiling at him.

'I haven't heard that name, Nathaniel, in a while. You do know my name is Mohammed, right? Mohammed Bilal, to be precise,' he says, grinning cheekily.

'Sorry, Mohammed. I didn't know you'd changed your name,' I reply, still smiling. 'When did that happen? What did your mum say?' I ask, thinking of her – a devoted Christian who never missed a Sunday service at Vicar William's church. She'd been attending for as long as I could remember, always dressed in her best with her Bible in hand.

'On the day I took my Shahada. The day I officially converted to Islam,' he says, his voice steady. He doesn't mention his mum.

Standing beside Mohammed, observing his unwavering commitment to his faith and his incredible journey to embrace Islam, I feel a deep admiration. Just as I am about to express my pride in him, an all-encompassing sound surrounds me, drawing me into profound awe. The call to prayer is a harmonious and enchanting tradition that moves me deeply, evoking a sense of wonder and appreciation for its beauty. I watch as a group of diverse men, each carrying prayer mats under their arms, begin to line up outside the mosque. Mohammed explains that he has to go to pray, and leaves me to join the group entering the mosque.

The distinctive architectural designs and elegant oval-shaped windows add to the sense of reverence and peace, I feel. I wait outside as Mohammed completes Jummah, and try calling Jacks on his mobile several times, but he doesn't respond. Growing frustrated, I keep calling until Mohammed emerges from the mosque, bringing relief. He says goodbye to an elder with a long grey beard and a taqiyah hat. His respectful tone and slight bow display cultural richness and respect. He looks completely refreshed and energized after the prayer.

'Sorry I took so long. I was seeking advice from the Imam,' he says.

I wonder whether he's ever shared his past life on road with the Imam or talked about what led him to convert to Islam. I ask, and he tells me the Imam never asked about his past – and that, honestly, it feels good just to be accepted by his Muslim brothers.

As Mohammed continues to share his deep thoughts about Islam, his phone suddenly rings, cutting our conversation short. I can't make out the caller's words, but I don't need to – his expression says it all. The warmth drains from his face, his smile fades, his jaw tightens and his eyes sharpen with a familiar intensity.

'They ain't drawing me out,' he says, his voice tense, as he ends the call with a sharp press of his thumb.

As we walk toward the Cotch, I notice his breathing getting heavier. His footsteps hit the ground harder, more purposefully. In this moment, the calm, collected Mohammed fades – and old Nathanial, the one shaped by the roads, starts to show again. It reminds me how fragile change really is. Even when someone's made it out, the past is never far away. Sometimes, all it takes is one phone call to drag them right back in.

I step in front of him, raising my hand to get his attention. 'What's going on?' I ask, a bit out of breath.

'It's dem man saying they're riding out, asking if I'm coming.' His expression twists – part disbelief, part frustration. 'How can they ask me such a foolish question, knowing man is on his Deen?' he adds, shaking his head. I can see him struggling to stay composed, his fists clenched tightly at his sides. 'Jacks's attack is stirring the mandem up, bringing the olders out of hibernation,' Mohammed mutters, wiping sweat from his forehead. 'But I'm not about to get involved, even though he's family.'

'Just take a deep breath,' I say gently, not sure if my voice is steady enough to calm him. 'They're just reacting out of anger. They're not thinking clearly right now.' Deep down, I admire his strong commitment to his faith, especially when there's so much pressure to retaliate when a friend or family member is violated.

'I told the mandem to focus on their Deen, but they aren't listening. Some of them have taken their Shahada, but they are still caught up in badness. But not me; I remain strong in my faith,' he declares, his hands trembling, still clearly upset.

'Mohammed, let's sit down and talk,' I say, nodding towards the bench in the park between the mosque and the

Cotch. It feels like the perfect place – calm and hidden away from the hustle and bustle.

We sit quietly for a moment, enjoying the warm sun on our backs and the cheerful sound of children laughing nearby. I let the moment breathe before easing into the question that's been on my mind.

'I wanted to ask about your spiritual journey,' I say carefully. 'I really admire how much you've evolved. Leaving the roads, your friends, all of that – it couldn't have been easy. What made you change?'

He looks at me, a mix of sadness and relief in his eyes. His words hit me right in the chest as he begins, 'Life on road isn't all it's cracked up to be. It's just one big trap that sells you dreams and then spits you out. You're just lost on road.'

He pauses, searching for the right words, then adds, 'Islam is the truth – it's a beautiful religion that helped me see things in the grand scale of things.'

I watch him closely, noticing how his shoulders seem to relax slightly as he opens up. He tells me how, before finding Islam, he used to take his problems out on the roads, acting recklessly and without direction. 'I didn't know what I was doing from one day to the next,' he admits quietly. 'But when I found Islam everything made sense. I became calm, at peace with myself. I wasn't stressed or in pain any more. You get me? Now, all I worry about is the Five Pillars and the Creator. I've submitted to the will of Allah.'

As he speaks, his voice low and steady, he reflects on the darker days – each word weighted with the heaviness of past struggles. 'When I was on road, I was selling drugs, getting into trouble with other mandem and the boydem. I nearly lost my life a couple of times – seen that white light flash right in front of me. My life was one big hot mess. I just felt hopeless.'

His honesty catches me off guard, and I find myself leaning in, hanging on every word. 'Life on road is a lie you tell yourself. You pretend you're all good, but, deep down, many mandem are desperate for change. That was me. I didn't want to live another day without purpose.'

I ask gently, 'What do you mean by lacking purpose?'

He looks away for a moment, his voice softer now. 'I was doing things with no real reason. Living for other people, for the roads. Getting stripes, thinking the mandem would rate me. But, thinking about it now, it was stupid. I didn't know who I was. I thought, this can't be all there is to life – there must be something else.'

His words hang, charged with meaning. 'When you're in the hood, on road, you're not free; you're trapped in all the madness. I just wanted peace. I saw brothers convert to Islam, but I wasn't interested back then – I was all about the roads. Not that I'm old now.' He chuckles, breaking the heaviness for a moment.

He admits he'd had enough of living on the edge. 'Getting into trouble, no direction. Being on road made me start thinking, innit. I used to wake up and think, why am I here? Why am I living? That's when I looked to other aspects to find the answer. In a way, that's why I turned to Islam. Since taking my Shahada, I haven't looked back.'

I find Mohammed's unique journey of spiritual development intriguing. His transformation not only offers hope but also sheds light on what Islam provides for a generation of young men navigating the struggles on road.

In recent years, there has been extensive discussion about reversion in prisons. Many government reports have addressed this issue, particularly a significant report from the Ministry of Justice in 2021.[2] Media outlets, including the *Telegraph*, have prominently featured discussions on the themes of radicalization and imprisonment.

For young men like Mohammed, the journey of Islamic conversion was not a path toward radicalization. Instead, it involved discovering a more profound sense of faith and spirituality. This transformation did not occur within the confines of prison walls either; instead, it took place on road, also synonymous with freedom being taken away. It was clear that Mohammed's criminality and marginalized situation forced him to question who he was, while the Islamic doctrine was described as opening new ways of perceiving his social world and his place within it.

As I sit next to Mohammed in the park, he keeps calling Jacks, checking his phone between each attempt, and clearly getting frustrated.

I decide to ask him: 'How has your life changed since becoming more religious?'

'It's a beautiful religion,' he replies simply. 'Helped me live clean. Took me away from all the madness on road.'

Curious, I ask if he feels at peace now.

Mohammed pauses, looking away as if he's weighing up his own thoughts. He seems to struggle to put it into words, but what he eventually says confirms what I've sensed – that Islam offers him a sense of clarity and direction he hadn't experienced before.

'Yeah, I do,' he says at last. 'When I read the Quran deeply, I realized my life had purpose. I just didn't find the truth until

I started to learn from the teachings. It shows you the purpose of life in a basic form straightforwardly.'

His eyes light up, and I'm drawn into the depths of his story. His spiritual journey seems worlds away from the struggle and survival that defined his old secular life. It's genuinely moving to observe someone seeking faith for salvation, yearning for tranquillity amidst the surrounding chaos.

Mohammed's voice grows more reflective as he continues. 'When you are on road you're not thinking about the Creator. You have no acknowledgement of God and the sacrifices that he made for you. It's all about giving into your desires on road, getting the P, hurting people. It's a selfish way to live. I'm at peace with my close relationship to God and abiding by his teachings. Islam showed me a different way; it accepted me, even with my flaws.'

I sit in deep thought, starting to grasp why Mohammed and some of his friends turned to Islam – searching for an escape from the toxic, traumatic effects of the roads.

After sitting on the bench for about thirty minutes, Mohammed suddenly leaps up. 'Jacks finally replied to my text! Come on, let's go!' We leave the comfort of the park and walk toward the Cotch.

A white car with a group of men drives slowly beside us, startling Mohammed and making him quicken his pace. I ask if he's okay, sensing his unease.

'I'm good,' he says, 'but a man's soul can never rest.' Though he's off the roads, hypervigilance still lingers.

The person in the car nods at Mohammed through the window and says, 'You good, akh?' After the car speeds off, Mohammed tells me that the driver stabbed his cousin when they were teenagers, and he still feels angry about it. But his faith has helped him decide against seeking revenge. This moment really makes me think about how violence leaves deep scars that stay with you long after it happens, and how the recall to violence is always bubbling under the surface, even when someone has stepped away from that life.

When we arrive at the Cotch, there's a large group of people standing around. The only person I recognize is Curtis who was friends with Jacks back in school. Jacks was always so popular when we were kids, but I'm shocked at the number of people prepared to ride out for him; it's more than I expected.

Mohammed greets Curtis with a firm handshake. '*As-salaam alaikum.*'

Curtis raises his eyebrows in surprise when he sees that Mohammed has joined them. He quickly asks what Mohammed is doing here, and Mohammed replies that he isn't 'riding out'. Curtis seems relieved and explains that the mandem had been blowing up his phone since early morning, but he doesn't want to get involved – he left the roads behind a couple of years ago and is now focused on his job. Mohammed then advises Curtis to go home to his wife and kids.

As I step into the living room, I find Jacks seated on the sofa with a massive spliff in hand. He's staring out of the window at the two magpies sitting on the fence. Judging by the smell of weed that hits me as I walk in, Leanne isn't home. His blue jogging bottoms are torn, and his yellow jumper is stained with drops of dried blood. He doesn't greet me as usual – no smile, no warmth. He's withdrawing from me as I sit beside him on the sofa.

Aron is pacing up and down, Cassius is shouting on

the phone, and Ash and Anthony are also spiralling – I am drawn to Jacks. It's as if the noise momentarily fades, and my focus narrows down to just us. I struggle to find the right words beyond the usual, 'Are you all right?' or, 'How are you feeling?' I already know the answer to those questions.

Instead, I lean in and whisper in his ear: 'I'm here for you.' What I meant to say is, 'I've been a nervous wreck since hearing about what happened to you. I'm so sorry that you've suffered another blow to the psyche. I'm so worried about how you'll handle this. I care about you so much,' but I didn't know how to convey that.

Our conversation at the trap house last month keeps flashing through my mind. I remember how lost Jacks seemed when he confided in me about not being happy and his struggle to fill the void he was feeling. He was all over the place, trying to comprehend being robbed. Now, with this being the second violation he's faced this month, I know it's only going to compound his stress. I'm worried that this will tip him over the edge and push him further into a lifestyle he desperately wants to escape.

My thoughts race as he glares at me; his eyes express unbearable sadness that hurts my heart. He mutters something inaudible to himself while pinching and squeezing the wound on his head. His mind seems scattered as he jumps from one concern to another, asking about Nia, his mum, his car and why I'm here. His big, expressive eyes look lost as he rocks back and forth on the sofa. He's mentally breaking down right in front of me, and this horrifies me. I hold him tight as he quietly says, 'I didn't even do anything; these kids violated me.'

Jacks looks through me as he speaks, still fixated on the

window and the scenery outside. What was once a bright summer day has transformed into night right before our eyes. Suddenly, he's recounting the terrifying ordeal he experienced. It feels like I'm watching a movie as he describes getting hit in the head, falling to the floor and facing a boy who was about to stab him. He managed to kick the boy, get up and run through the estate, feeling weightless. He was exhausted, unable to scream, his clothes soaked in sweat and blood as he hid behind the wheelie bins, wondering if Neil was dead. Finally, he reached Cassius's house and collapsed on the floor.

I gaze at him and ask, 'Jacks, you're not planning to retaliate, are you?' He sighs and slumps back on the sofa in frustration as if my question is the silliest thing he's ever heard.

'What am I supposed to do?' he asks quietly.

I remind him about his little girl, and I let the silence linger for a moment. Then, I notice that he's crying, not loudly or dramatically, but quietly weeping, his shoulders trembling. This time, I don't attempt to console him. The mention of Nia always brings Jacks to tears, but I understand that he needs to release his emotions and consider how his actions will impact her.

'Jacks, come, let's go home. Auntie Grace is going out of her mind with worry,' Mohammed finally speaks to Jacks, with nervousness I haven't seen before.

'Mohammed, you shouldn't be here. Has prayer finished? I don't want you involved,' Jacks says, wiping the tears from his eyes. This is the first time I can see glimpses of Jacks returning to himself, his care and protection evident for his younger cousin, which is what Jacks is known for.

'I ain't leaving this house without you, my brother, and I ain't letting any of the mandem draw you out and convince you to mess up your life,' Mohammed says with a forceful intensity that silences the commotion in the room.

'What's up, Mohammed? You can't expect us to let this slide. I know you're on your Deen, but you know how the roads go. If we back down, they'll just keep coming,' Anthony interjects, turning to Mohammed, with a look of concern.

'You man are supposed to be on your Deen too. Why can't you just have faith and walk with Allah?' Mohammed says, his voice cracking. His words are a drop-the-mic moment as everyone looks around, unsure what to say.

Even though Mohammed is surrounded by his childhood friends, he and they are on different paths. There's a clear strain between him and his former best friend, Ash, who hasn't made any effort to engage with him since we arrived. The group seem uneasy around Mohammed – likely because they deeply respect him, not just as a former predatory trapper and badman, but now as a devoted convert. His presence unsettles them; they want to change too, but wrestle with the pull of the roads. The atmosphere during this reunion is thick with unspoken tension.

'Yo, my G,' Ash finally speaks up, grinning widely. The joy of the long-awaited reunion lights up his face. 'It's been too long,' he says, stepping in to give Mohammed a firm handshake.

'Yeah, it's been a minute. Wish it was under better circumstances,' Mohammed responds, pulling Ash in for a hug as they shake hands. The warmth of their embrace brings a quiet sense of nostalgia and joy, gently easing the tension in the room.

I love witnessing the heartfelt reunion of old friends. Yet, I'm struck by the stark contrast between Mohammed's spiritual journey and that of his former best friend and most of the group.

But the brief calm doesn't last long. The serene moment is abruptly interrupted by Anthony. 'When are we rolling out, lads?' he says, stirring up the group again.

As I look around, I see a mix of emotions on everyone's faces. Some show signs of anger, while others seem confused. Deep down, I can sense their hesitation, the unspoken fear of taking the risk. Each person seems to be battling their own thoughts and fears, their inner tension visible in their tense postures. It's obvious that everyone is imagining different outcomes in their minds. Sitting with them, I feel an overwhelming need to shout to tell them to stop, to save themselves before it goes wrong. But, instead, I hold my breath, feeling the suffocating tension in the room, knowing that the choice isn't mine to make.

And then comes an unexpected statement from Mohammed: 'My brothers, it's time to pray.' The room falls silent once again. Without hesitation, Mohammed, Anthony and Aron swiftly remove their trainers and socks and prepare for prayer. As they leave the room, brother to brother, I can tell they are determined to pray. Their shared faith immediately acts as a unifying force, bringing them together in a moment of spiritual connection amidst the surrounding call to violence.

'I've been thinking about converting to Islam,' Jacks says with a smile that feels genuine, unlike how he was acting earlier. 'That's why I was at the mosque earlier. I was gonna go in, but chose not to, because I don't think I'm completely ready to make the change,' he explains, while scratching his head. There's a noticeable shift in his energy as if the thought of finding his faith is already a positive change within him. It's a hopeful sign that he's moving away from his earlier obsession with getting revenge.

'Mohammed is always telling me about how Islam saved him and made his heart clean and put his soul at rest,' Jacks explains. 'Do you know how badly I wanna feel at peace? I don't wanna have all these demons running around in my head. I don't wanna think about violence, who will attack man, and if man should retaliate. Mohammed doesn't have these battles any more: he's asked for forgiveness, he's cleansed his sins, he's found redemption,' he says, taking a deep pull from his cigarette.

I nod, understanding his struggle. As his childhood friend, I've witnessed his ongoing battle with deep depression and dark thoughts for as long as I can remember, so I empathize with the tremendous burden he carries. Jacks has begun scratching his eczema, indicating that his mind is working overtime, processing his recent negative experiences while on road. This theme of redemption is a central topic in our conversation. It's a struggle that many men like Jacks face – a battle with their past and a strong desire for a fresh start, a clean slate. I've often heard the mandem describe their road identities using metaphors such as stained and tainted with the badman identity characterized by mental turmoil. Those who recognized the fragility of their road identities were embarking on a deeply personal journey of redemption. Their focus is to nurture a more positive and respectable self-image while striving to break free from the constraints of their former badman identities. Jacks appears to be deeply immersed in a quest for absolution from his past transgressions. He's seeking inner peace and personal growth, realizing that he cannot find these things within the confines of his current lifestyle.

As I glance up at the clock, watching its hand inch forward, I realize I've been at the Cotch for over four hours. The crowd outside has thinned, and Mohammed, Aron and Anthony have finished their prayers and left in Ash's car to grab some takeaway. Even though I know I should leave, I feel a deep concern pushing me to stay close to Jacks. I want to support him as he processes his emotions, hoping that by staying close I can prevent him from giving in to thoughts of revenge. I know I can't control his actions, but listening to him and sharing the burden of his emotional struggles has also helped me sort through my own feelings about the terrible attack he's experienced.

A heavy numbness settles in my chest, mixed with an unfamiliar simmer of anger bubbling beneath the surface. Jacks is caught up in the chaos of postcode wars, despite having no personal stake in it. He's a big man, yet a target for boys barely old enough to grasp the gravity of their actions. Each new generation pushes boundaries further, taking things too far year after year, attacking anyone who fits the mould of their perceived enemy.

It deeply saddens me that these young boys can't see the humanity in Jacks or in themselves. They are blinded by a strong desire for revenge, like a fire that destroys everything it touches, leaving behind only the ashes of lost potential. They are trapped in an endless cycle of anger and hostility, each mirroring the other's suffering. Instead of finding common ground and solidarity, they turn on each other, revealing their worst sides under the pressure of shared struggles on road. I feel hopeless when I think about this violence. Will the cycle of pain and retaliation ever end?

I sit quietly with Jacks as he finishes his call with his mother. His voice is steady, even though he feels turmoil inside himself. He tried to be strong and hold things together for her sake, ever the caregiver and always putting her needs above his own. Watching his quiet resilience, I wish for a glimmer of hope in all this darkness.

Aron, Mohammed, Ash and Anthony re-enter the living room just after 9 p.m., breaking through our emotional moment. They each carry a plastic bag filled with aromas of Caribbean takeout. It feels surreal how the tumultuous events of the past few hours seemed to dissipate into the air, making way for a sense of tranquil normalcy as they prepared to enjoy a comforting meal after their prayer. Cassius wakes up from his nap on the sofa, groggy.

'Did we take long?' Ash asks. His demeanour has changed, and I can tell Mohammed's return has a lot to do with his shift in mood and the more positive atmosphere overall. 'Man had to remind Mohammed of what he is missing, being in the sticks with no culture or proper food,' he says, laughing loudly.

'We got your favourite, jerk chicken,' Aron chimes in, handing me a clean plate and fork.

Mohammed turns to Jacks with a comforting tone: 'I told Curtis and dem man to head home. You're not going anywhere, my brother, except to your bed.' He smiles warmly and adds, 'Smash into this ackee and saltfish. I'll drive you home later. I think I'll stay the night. It's been too long since I've seen Nia and Auntie.'

We all enjoy our meal together, savouring every bite of our delicious food. As we conversed for hours, exchanging lively good-natured banter, one remark that Mohammed had made earlier stayed with me. He had raised a thought-provoking question about his friends' commitment to their faith. This comment sparks my curiosity, prompting me to reflect on the internal struggles faced by Aron, Cassius and Anthony as they navigate their religious lives while dealing with toxic experiences on road. I raise this with Mohammed as we all sit.

'Earlier you mentioned that the mandem should also be on their Deen. What did you mean by that?'

'Come on, man, let's just chill now. Only you would remember something like that,' Cassius replies with a forced laugh.

Mohammed falls silent. Sensing his unease, I decide not to press for answers, allowing the weight of his unspoken thoughts to settle over the group. Then Anthony, known for his ability to dispel awkward silences, breaks the quiet with a thought-provoking reply:

'The mandem haven't taken enough time to understand Islam,' he explains.

'So much man are calling themselves an "akh", but ask any of them if they know why they turned to Islam, they wouldn't be able to give you an answer. Not all the mandem go mosque. Mandem are still keeping up badness, still clubbing, smoking Some man even eat pork – that's haram,' he adds, shaking his head.

I can sense Anthony's frustration. Even though he is speaking about his peers in the third person, he is clearly describing his struggles to practise his faith. What stands out, and I am surprised to learn, is the varying levels of commitment to Islam within the group, which I wasn't aware of before. In the group, Mohammed is widely recognized as a devoted pilgrim and a transformed individual. On the other hand, it is clear that Anthony and some others are alternating between their day-to-day lives on road and particular aspects of Islamic tradition and practice. I started to perceive this approach as a 'pick-and-mix' version of Islam, where their religion isn't supplanting their road identity, but, rather, is an extension of it. I express my wonder out loud, wanting to hear more of the mandem's thoughts. Immediately, there's a collective reaction of audible sighs and shifts in body language. They're not escaping the question, but rather thinking of a way to answer it truthfully and engage in our discussion intently.

Anthony takes a deep breath before speaking. He seems calm, but chooses his words carefully. He talks about how Islam has given him structure and discipline – something solid to hold on to, but, even with that, he admits his struggles are far from over.

'Mohammed was able to leave – that's why he's on it. Me? I still feel the pressure. The roads have me up. I just haven't put as much time into Islam as I have into this lifestyle.' He shifts in his chair, his discomfort clear in the way his hands tighten on his knees.

Cassius nods slowly, biting his lip, as he looks around the room. He shares that he tries to stay on his Deen, but living around here – 'still seeing the same fuckery' – makes it hard to stay focused. He pulls a cigarette from his pocket and flicks it to Jacks, who is soaking in every word.

Mohammed relaxes on the sofa, hands resting loosely in

his lap. He's listening intently to his friends, showing a new kind of humility, a sharp contrast to the alpha he once was, dominating every conversation.

Aron finally speaks up, his words heavy with truth. 'Islam was my only hope. But it's hard to change completely. It's a battle, man. Islam only helped me to a certain degree. The roads – it's all I know, all I know how to do.'

Turning to Aron, Mohammed reassures him: 'Allah is with you, my brother; he'll guide you. I won't tell you how to live your life, but the path to Allah is the one true way.' Touched by these words, Aron rises, extends his hand to Mohammed, and softly replies, 'Insha'Allah.'

As the conversation goes on, Mohammed's words grow more passionate, emphasizing the personal fulfilment that comes from committing to faith – a fulfilment waiting for those on road who manage to break free from their former lifestyles. His message carries hope, highlighting the potential for change even in the most challenging circumstances. His friends listen closely, completely absorbed.

Jacks, visibly moved, pauses for a moment before turning to Mohammed with determination. 'Tomorrow, I've made up my mind to go back to the mosque and have a conversation with the Imam to ask more questions about Islam.'

Cassius quickly chimes in, saying he wants to go too.

Mohammed nods, acknowledging their decisions, and offers to go with them. With that, he bids a heartfelt farewell to his friends just after 1 a.m. Feeling sad, Ash realizes that this reunion with his closest friend might be the last time he sees Mohammed unless Jacks needs him again.

The next day, I meet up with Jacks, fresh from the mosque. I'd hoped Cassius would be with him, but, knowing Cassius's track record with promises, I'm not surprised he isn't. Jacks lets out a frustrated sigh and rubs his tired eyes. He says he rang Cassius three times this morning, but each call went to voicemail, so eventually he gave up.

'He's not serious about being on his Deen,' Jacks says flatly.

The sun is out this afternoon, and the sky is soft and blue. For a moment, time feels slower. I zoom in on Jacks's face. He has dark circles under his eyes, indicating that he hasn't been sleeping well since the incident two days ago.

As we walk towards his car, he keeps his hood up even though it's warm outside. We wave at Mrs Paula, who hurries into her house with bags of shopping.

'How're you feeling?' I ask.

He tries to brush it off. 'I'm fine.'

But I hear the strain in his voice and see him fidgeting. I slow down and step in front of him so he has to look at me – something he's been avoiding since we linked up.

'It's okay not to be okay,' I gently tell him.

He sidesteps me and keeps walking. 'I'm alright. I'd tell you if I wasn't,' but I can see doubt in his eyes. He's not deliberately lying – he just doesn't know how to admit the truth.

When we reach his car, he finally opens up a bit. Says he's been thinking about the violation, but tries to downplay it like it's just part of life now.

We stand outside the car for a bit before heading out of the estate for lunch. As we drive, his mood changes when the conversation turns to Mohammed. He tells me how proud he is of him – calls him 'an inspiration', someone who's where he wants to be: free from the trap.

I nod in agreement. Yesterday was the first time I've seen Mohammed since he converted to Islam. I noticed a calmness in him, a new confidence. Islam has given him peace and purpose – a framework to navigate his past and face his future.

When I ask Jacks if he's planning to convert, he hesitates before admitting that he's not quite ready. He's spoken with the Imam and a few brothers at the mosque, and their words resonated with him, but he feels he needs more time to figure out if it's the right path for him.

We spend the drive to Jacks's favourite Turkish restaurant talking about faith, prayer, spirituality and what life could look like beyond the roads. As we leave the familiar surroundings behind, I can sense a change in Jacks – it's as if he can finally breathe a little easier, without the weight of the world on him.

As we cruise down a street lined with beautiful houses, he says, 'Life has to mean more than this. My life has to mean more than this, right?' Then, almost in a whisper, he adds, 'I have to get out.'

There's something in his voice – not quite hope, but the beginning of it. He's starting to picture a different life, one that's peaceful. Maybe something like Mohammed's. Even though it's buried under layers of pain and chaos, the hope – it's there.

This is where change really begins. Not with fireworks or loud declarations, but with quiet, almost fragile moments – whispered confessions and tiny shifts in perspective. Jacks is still deep in his struggles, still locked in a life that pulls him back in again and again. But maybe, just maybe, he's found his first way out – by letting himself imagine something better.

For now, as he shares his dreams, he seems at peace. But I know Jacks has a long and difficult journey ahead – one that involves breaking free both physically and mentally from the roads that continue to hold him captive.

CHAPTER 6

Pen

It's a chilly winter morning and nearly Christmas. I'm walking to Vinnie's corner shop, admiring how much the community has embraced the festive season, with the numerous decorations in the windows, which light up the grey morning. Mr Wilson from number 29 has gone all out, decorating his three front windows with beautiful wreaths and hanging festive mistletoe on the front door. A stunning Christmas tree with twinkling lights, candy canes and silver, red and green ornaments stands proudly at the front entrance of his house. A large inflatable reindeer is perched on the wheelie bin, playing joyful Christmas tunes. It reminds me of the movie *Home Alone*. Strolling along the green outside Vinnie's, Mrs Paula walks her beloved Yorkshire terrier, Millie, dressed in a vibrant red Father Christmas jumper. Her bright eyes and warm smile instantly lift my spirits.

'Ebony! Come around for some fruit cake when you get a chance.'

I smile and am about to respond when I hear an all too familiar sound overhead. Our joyful expressions to one another turn into confusion as we look up at the sky and see a loud helicopter overhead, its noise growing louder and more oppressive by the second as it hovers above. I say goodbye and turn the corner to see what brought the helicopter to

Northville, and my holiday spirit is shattered by the chaotic gathering outside Andy's house. Among the crowd, I make out his mother, Shelly, and his sister Bella still in her pyjamas, animatedly speaking on the phone, but her words are lost in the chatter of the onlookers. As I draw closer, her voice becomes more distinct.

'They took Andy. The police kicked down the door early this morning and arrested him,' she sobs.

I see the shattered front door from the police's battering ram, and inside I glimpse Shelly seated in the living room, visibly shaken, smoking a cigarette.

She doesn't hear me ask her a question, instead focused on her phone conversation. 'How could this happen now? He was going to college, trying to better himself.'

As Bella continues her restless pacing, Cassius appears, his dark hoodie pulled low over his head. He lingers behind Bella's car and scans the street like a hawk. I can tell he's nervous.

'Cassius, what's happened?' I ask.

'It's a madness. I need to go and talk to Auntie Shelly.'

Shelly emerges from the house, commanding everyone to move from her door. The crowd disperses, no one daring to question her authority in this crisis.

Cassius's nervousness becomes understandable as he is the one that tells her the truth.

'Auntie Shelly, Andy has been nabbed for drug dealing. I swear, I didn't think it would go this far. I just linked him with someone I knew – that's all.'

Cassius's anxiety is justified – he isn't merely a messenger. He had helped Andy make the connection. Just one introduction, he'd told himself. But it all went left: now Andy is in custody, and the burden of that decision weighs heavily on him.

I'm stunned by Cassius's blunt confession, but I understand his need to be honest in this moment. He's always urged the mandem 'not to be fake' around their families, to be open about their lives on road. Yet, he's the only one in the group who actually follows his own advice. As far as Andy's family knew, despite facing challenges in secondary school he was now in college, working towards a qualification in the technical field.

Shelly turns to her daughter her face like thunder. 'Did you know about this?' and Cassius hastily bows out of view, sensing the looming storm.

'Of course, I didn't know. If you spent more time asking him about his life and how he's feeling, maybe he would open up to you more,' Bella snaps, but the regret in her eyes is evident as soon as the words leave her lips.

Shelly remains silent for a moment. I can feel her emotions simmering beneath the surface before she finally erupts. She hurls her coffee mug at the outside wall, the hot liquid splattering on all of us, and storms back inside in abrupt fury. Bella's hands tremble at her mother's outburst, as she turns to me and offers to wipe my jeans.

'Don't worry about that, Bella. It's not important. What can I do to help?' I reassure her, drawing her close and placing my arms around her shoulders.

'Mum is just upset, and with her depression she just doesn't know how to handle high-stress situations. I shouldn't have said that to her. It will only make her feel worse. I'm just all over the place. How can Andy put us through this? I need to get to him and see if he's okay.'

Despite Bella being five years older than her brother, she often plays the role of a mother to him and their cousin, Aron. She is a born nurturer and feels a strong sense of responsibility towards her family. Bella turns round and goes to see her mother, while Cassius and I decide to continue my walk towards Vinnie's so we can talk.

'This wasn't supposed to happen. Man was just looking to make some extra P. He told me he was only gonna trap for a bit and now look at this mess,' Cassius recounts. His phone rings repeatedly, and he puts it on mute.

'Man was trying to bring him in.'

I listen intently to Cassius, pondering how Andy concealed his double life from Bella, the detective, known for her sharp intuition. It's hard to believe that he managed to keep his drug dealing a secret for so long, especially with her talent for finding the truth.

'Andy is gonna go mad in pen. He's too used to being home with his family,' Cassius says sadly as we leave Vinnie's. 'I've been in and out of prison, and it's no joke. It's tough not having any freedom. I feel guilty, man,' he confesses.

I'm interested in Cassius's reflections on his experience in prison and take the opportunity to delve deeper into his story, recognizing the all-too-frequent encounters young men in Northville face with the criminal justice system.

'How many times have you been to prison?' I enquire, curious about how conversations about being nabbed and going pen have become a distressingly regular part of their lives by the time they reach their teenage years.

'I've lost count, man, but that's nothing to be proud of,' he replies. 'I got in trouble with the boydem when I was around thirteen. I was accused of robbing my classmate's phone, but

I swear I didn't do it.' A hint of distress crosses his face as he recalls that day.

'They came to my house. I remember it like it was yesterday. They slapped handcuffs on me. Can you believe that? Man was just a yout, but they didn't see me like that. They stereotype you just because of where we live,' he adds. 'I never thought I'd be caught up with them. I watched my uncles, when I was younger, being harassed by the boydem, lined up against the wall like some criminals. These times, Uncle Jazzy was a big-time businessman; he wasn't involved in anything dodgy.' He shakes his head as old memories come back to him.

'All I've seen is the police harassing the mandem, and then they wonder why we don't like them,' he says, his voice laced with bitterness.

'What happened during your first arrest?' I ask, bringing the conversation back to his first encounter with the police.

'They gave me probation. What a joke, just for being on the bus when a kid got robbed. From that day, I couldn't take these people seriously. I knew I'd always be seen as a target in their eyes – a criminal. Well, that's how it felt,' he adds, the memory clearly still stinging.

We walk back to Bella's house, and Cassius prepares to light his spliff when he notices two police community-support officers questioning young boys in the distance. Cassius walks in the opposite direction without hesitation, and I struggle to catch up with him.

'I ain't getting nabbed for a spliff. That plastic police, the one who looks like Peter from *Family Guy*, is always harassing the mandem. The other fed he's with is cool, though. He's always asking how my mum is, but I'm not taking any chances with the other one; he'll call out the bully van and get man nabbed,' he explains.

'Cassius, slow down,' I call after him, realizing that seeing the police often triggers a reflexive response in him – to run – regardless of whether he has done anything wrong. This reaction is all too familiar for many black boys, shaped by a troubled relationship with the police, characterized by constant profiling and damaging stereotypes that paint black men as perpetual criminals.

These harmful prejudices and misconceptions are propagated through various media outlets, including the news, which often sensationalizes incidents involving Black men. This constant exposure to negative portrayals fosters an environment where assumptions of guilt overshadow the presumption of innocence. As a result, complex issues are often oversimplified, leading to biased interpretations.

Reflecting on this harsh reality, I consider society's quickness to stereotype, which hampers the police officers' ability to see these young people as anything more than the sum of their criminal activities. This blindness prevents them from recognizing the human beings behind the labels. Generations of young men and boys in Northville and across the country have grappled with systemic challenges beyond their control, struggling to overcome them. These deeply ingrained obstacles contribute to many becoming trapped in the revolving door of the criminal justice system, with no end in sight.

We make it to Shelly's house and see mother and daughter coming out of the front door. Shelly is holding a plate wrapped in foil, and the smell is instantly recognizable – it's pepper steak, her son's favourite dish. She's also holding a large bottle of Fanta, another of his favourites.

'Andy just called, and we know which police station they've taken him to,' Bella says, strapping her daughter Jessie in her car seat.

'I'm rolling . . . I mean, I'm coming along too,' Cassius declares, seeking Shelly's approval. She remains silent, but Bella gives him permission, cautioning him to wait outside in case the police are looking for him.

Cassius reassures her, saying, 'If they were after me, they would have kicked down my mum's door by now.'

We arrive at the police station just after 2 p.m. Shelly's hands tremble, causing her to drop the bottle of Fanta on the floor. Jessie picks it up and holds her grandma's hand tightly as we pass several police vans and enter the police station through the automatic doors. The waiting area is cold and clinical, with blue iron chairs, white walls, and cream doors. On the sealed plastic notice board are posters about restorative justice, drink driving and fraud prevention.

'I've come to collect my son,' Shelly tells the police officer at the information desk. He makes a call and then informs Shelly that the duty solicitor is with Andy and will come out to see her soon.

'How is my son?' Shelly enquires. 'Can you bring him this plate of food, please?' she adds.

'Sorry, that won't be possible,' the police officer responds, routinely ignoring Shelly's first question about her son's well-being. 'Please take a seat. The solicitor will be with you soon,' he adds, his frustration evident as he tries to calm a man who has had too much to drink and is asking about his daughter in custody.

In the cold waiting area, Cassius attempts to inject some lightheartedness with a few inappropriate jokes to pass the time. As we wait, Andy's extended family and friends arrive one by one. Andy's dad, Lenny; Aron and his older brother Zak; Ash; Andy's girlfriend, Beth; and two of Beth's friends all join us in the waiting area. Aron hugs his aunt tightly and holds Bella's hand while comforting her.

'Are you okay, Auntie Shelly? I'm sorry I couldn't get here sooner. I was at Shyanne's house this morning and came as soon as I found out.'

'You're here now,' she replies, her eyes fixed on Andy's dad. Shelly doesn't allow Lenny to even greet her before she shouts at him: 'Where have you been? I've been calling you for hours.' Her voice echoes, drawing the attention of the police officer at the front desk.

'I was at work and left as soon as I heard your voicemail,' he replies. His voice is always so calm that it makes it hard for anyone to be mad at him.

Andy's parents divorced years ago, but Lenny is still very involved in Andy and Bella's lives. He always attends family functions and readily offers support whenever his family need him. Lenny sits beside his granddaughter on the iron chair, easing his slight frame into the seat. He removes his worn brown flat cap, revealing his grey hair. He begins to roll a cigarette, and turns his attention to Cassius, who has been avoiding eye contact with Lenny since he arrived.

'Yout, why don't you and Andy go look a trade? England is the land of opportunity; England looks after you. It's not like my time when I had to wash cars, and there was so much prejudice. You have a chance now. Why don't you do something with your life?'

'I hear you, uncle,' Cassius whispers. The gravity of the situation has left him speechless. As Lenny pours out his emotions about his son's arrest, the room fills with a heavy silence, broken only by the occasional shuffling of Jessie's feet and her tired cries.

'Why did this yout have to get caught up with the police?' Lenny asks, overwhelmed, as he covers his face and leans back in the chair. 'I've never been in trouble with the law, and I raised him better than this,' he continues. 'I can't stop worrying about how my son is coping without us,' he adds, glancing at Shelly. She sees his distress and sits beside him.

Throughout the conversation, Cassius keeps his gaze fixed on the ground, unable to meet Lenny's eyes. I can almost feel the shame radiating from him, his guilt pressing down on the room. It's clear why he is so reserved now - he worries that Lenny, Shelly, and Leanne will blame him. Leanne has always been his biggest supporter, and he fears disappointing her.

Time seems to pass incredibly slowly in the sterile waiting area, made even more uncomfortable by the harsh fluorescent lights. We watch a steady stream of worried people coming and going, each asking about their loved ones. Shelly, agitated and restless, gets up to go outside for another smoke when, suddenly, the heavy door separating the cells from the waiting area creaks open. A woman with tired eyes, revealing her long hours, balances a sleek black briefcase, a stack of paperwork and a steaming cup of coffee in her hands.

'Ms Warren,' she calls.

Shelly approaches the solicitor. 'Is my son okay?'

'Andy is doing okay. Unfortunately, it's not good news. He hasn't been granted bail, and he's being held on remand until the sentencing hearing. The charges against him are serious, and the evidence is damning.'

The gravity of the news doesn't quite hit Shelly, and she asks again, 'How is my son?'

Lenny gets up to hold on to Shelly, who is now shaking. The information about Andy being held on remand is still sinking in.

'I'm sorry, Ms Warren. Andy will be sent directly to prison,' the solicitor repeats.

This time, the news hits and the sound that comes out of Shelly's mouth is indescribable. Shelly's legs give way, and Lenny catches her in his arms. More tears and disbelief fill the room. Lenny manages to gather information from the solicitor about the seriousness of the charge.

According to the solicitor, Andy got caught up in a police operation where undercover officers posed as drug users to catch people selling drugs. The evidence against him was strong. One of the undercover officers claimed Andy had sold him drugs, and there was even talk of his alleged involvement in a gang.

It was hard to hear. But, deep down, we all knew Andy wasn't part of any drug gang. He was just a lost teenager who'd made a misguided choice to chase quick wealth. Now, he would face the consequences – and his family would too.

Bella springs into action, as she always does during a crisis. She approaches the solicitor and asks for a piece of paper and a pen. Determined, she starts collecting messages for Andy from everyone, not knowing when they will have the chance to see or speak to him again. When it's my turn to write, I hesitate, unsure of what to say. I notice touching messages from Aron, encouraging his cousin to keep his head up, and Beth pledging unwavering support. Shelly's note to her son is filled with love and signed off with multiple Xs. In contrast,

I write a short line, simply letting him know that I'm outside with his family and expressing my sadness for what has happened to him. Bella then takes the crumpled piece of paper and gives it to the solicitor, asking her to pass it on to Andy.

We leave the police station. Shelly can barely walk. Lenny is still supporting her. Bella's stoic facade barely conceals her emotions. Beth's cries are guttural, and Aron's cussing into his phone shows his anger. Cassius's emotions are a mystery as he stays distant during our walk to the car. Cassius and I don't speak a word on the journey home – the music is turned up loud, signalling his desire not to talk. I sit in quiet contemplation, pondering the events that led Andy to a situation that could irreversibly alter his future – a future we had all hoped would be bright and promising.

Two weeks pass before I see Bella and Cassius again. It's Christmas Eve and we're sitting in Shelly's warm living room, lit by the soft glow of Christmas lights, waiting for a call from Andy on his burner phone. Bella is dressed in her nightgown, her long, thick hair wrapped up in a bun. Worry lines crease her forehead, dimming her usual natural glow.

'I was reading a letter from Andy before you guys came. He writes as often as he can, and I do love hearing from him, but not being able to see him in person is so hard.' Her voice holds sadness as she shares Andy's letter with me.

The letter begins with 'Hello Big Sis', setting a personal tone as Andy pours out his heart. He expresses the weight of his feelings for her and Shelly, revealing his regret for burdening them with his troubles. The thought of being separated from his family during Christmas weighs heavily on him, and he shares how much he will miss the turkey leg – a cherished tradition that everyone saves for him.

As Andy reflects on his time inside, he shares the challenges he faces sharing a small cell with strangers, a struggle made worse by his obsession with cleanliness. This confinement amplifies his feelings of loneliness, especially at night when he feels even more isolated. He reveals that his rivals are on his wing, which makes him anxious about engaging in educational opportunities due to the fear of facing them alone.

Despite the difficulties he encounters while adjusting to life in prison, Andy concludes the letter on a positive note. He mentions his new friend Grant, another inmate who shares his faith and who is helping him stay out of trouble through their cooking lessons together.

Reading Andy's heartfelt letter, I can almost hear his voice coming through the page. His longing for home and his family is unmistakable. The weight of his imprisonment is heavy not just for him, but for those he loves. If only he could fully grasp the extent of the heartbreak his situation has caused for those dear to him. Bella, who used to be full of life, now struggles with sleeplessness and anxiety. Shelly moves through her days on autopilot, her spirit weighed down by the pain of losing her son, yet she quietly tries to heal. She keeps the household running, balances the demands of her job and supports Andy financially while he is locked up. Her strength and resilience shine through amid the heartbreak that suffocates her. Even Beth, his devoted girlfriend, faces her own challenges as she watches her university aspirations slip away. She constantly seeks reassurance and guidance on how to best support him.

Reflecting on these remarkable and strong women, I am

struck by their vital roles in Andy's life. They are nurturers and caregivers, silently bearing the emotional and physical burdens that stem from his choices, while heroically holding everything together. Andy is fortunate to have their support as he confronts the turmoil he has caused in their lives. There's a sense of regret in his words as he grapples with the consequences of his decisions and the ripple effects they have created for his family. Witnessing their struggles has been nothing short of heartbreaking, and I can only hope that he uses his time in prison to reflect and truly understand the damage caused by his absence and the love that still surrounds him despite it all.

I give the letter back to Bella, who carefully tucks it in the drawer under the TV. I'm concerned about how she's coping. I ask her how she's doing. She responds with a numbness that speaks to the harsh truth of Andy's imprisonment. She says life has come to a standstill since his arrest. Her mother's depression has deepened, made worse by her refusal to discuss it. Bella also worries about Aron, who has become increasingly withdrawn and hasn't even checked in with them. She feels alone and fears losing her job due to her multiple absences from work. As we sit together, I offer a listening ear as she anxiously awaits Andy's call.

Shortly after, Shelly joins us, serving glasses of sherry and Christmas pudding topped with cream, but the atmosphere remains heavy with unspoken concerns. Shelly is clearly in survival mode, moving mechanically through her household chores. Bella's phone starts ringing from an unknown number. She answers the call and puts it on loudspeaker so we can all listen. Bella repeatedly and, anxiously, calls out, 'Hello,' before we finally hear Andy's voice on the other end.

'What's good, family?' Andy whispers.

'Mum, Andy's on the phone. Come quick,' Bella calls out to Shelly.

In a flurry, Shelly races into the living room. 'Hello, son, how are you?' she says, tears streaming down her face, the relief evident in her voice.

'Don't cry, Mum. I'm doing okay. Miss you loads. How are you? Has the solicitor called you? I'm going to court soon. One sec. I think the screw is coming,' Andy whispers, and then the phone call abruptly ends.

Andy's quiet words, spoken in a hushed tone over the phone, are a lifeline for his family. His mum and sister cling to the connection he's provided in these uncertain times.

Bella sits on the edge of the sofa, nervously biting her nails and staring at the phone on the table as she anxiously waits for Andy to call back, but he never does.

'This is what I hate about all this! I can't just talk to him whenever I want,' she vents in frustration.

Cassius leans against the kitchen counter, another glass of sherry in his hand, trying to calm her down.

'Just chill, man, Bella. That's how it goes. He's using a burner phone – it might not even be his. He probably had to give it back to whoever he trusted it from,' he explains, trying to diffuse the tension in the room.

'I'm just so scared for him,' she confesses, her voice almost breaking. 'After reading what he said about being locked down with rivals, I'm more on edge. I keep calling Beth and crying, asking how he's holding up, because it seems like he talks to her more than me.'

Cassius lets out a heavy sigh, 'C'mon, fix up, man. That's his gal and she holding him down. He can't confide in you the way he does with her, as you'll only worry. We all know what you're like.'

Bella cuts her eye at him. 'Go easy with the sherry. You know you'll already in Mum's bad books. And stop chatting shit,' she continues, her voice raising slightly. 'I don't mean it that way at all. I'm not competing with Beth for his attention. I just want to talk to him more. What's wrong with that?'

Cassius shrugs nonchalantly, but his eyes are serious. 'All you need to know is that he will be fine in there. Many mandem from Northville are there with him – they'll protect him. Just relax and stop being a drama queen,' he teases.

I sit back and watch them bicker, as they usually do, each one trying to get the last word in. It's a familiar sight of competitive banter, a mix of love and irritation. If the situation weren't so sad, I would probably laugh at their antics, but I just sit there in silence, sensing the tension between friendship and worry crackling like electricity around us.

The new year comes and, with it, Andy's sentencing in March. The night before his date at the magistrates' court, everyone has been warned to dress in their finest to present a good image of Andy to the court. Shelly wanted to show that Andy came from a respectable, upstanding family. Lenny took the warning seriously, looking impeccable in a crisp pinstripe suit, bowler hat and polished shoes. Even Aron, who usually wears casual tracksuits, is wearing a smart shirt and trousers. It's a powerful display of their deep love for Andy.

'I need to find the barrister. I can't believe we haven't met him yet,' Shelly says, panicked.

'Calm down, love. We have another hour before we go

into court. Let's go and find him,' Lenny reassures Shelly, leading her towards the massive glass doors.

We form a line to pass through the security of the magistrate's court, emptying our pockets and bags into trays, taking off our coats and passing through the metal detectors before finally being patted down, which feels intensely intrusive. It's uncomfortable and makes me feel as if I'm a suspect.

Aron, Zak and Ash look visibly uncomfortable too as the security guard checks them with handheld scanners. In contrast, Lenny and Shelly are undeterred by the checks and are focused on finding the barrister. There's a flurry of activity inside. Families and barristers come and go, and the building buzzes with the energy of multiple cases taking place at once. The hectic activity only adds to the anxiety we all feel. The barrister finds Shelly in the middle of it all. He's a middle-aged white man with brown hair dressed in a long black gown, a white shirt and a wig. He seems preoccupied, with a thousand thoughts racing through his mind.

'I'll be representing Andy today,' he says. 'Can we take a moment to have a brief discussion?' and he guides Shelly and Lenny to a quieter area.

Here, Shelly explains how tirelessly she works to care for her family and the struggles she and her son have faced with depression. She explains the challenges of parenting young boys in an area rife with postcode wars and drugs, emphasizing her unwavering efforts to instil good morals in Andy despite their environment. Shelly also speaks passionately about her daughter Bella's credible career in human resources. It seems she's trying to prove to the barrister that they are people of value, hoping to prevent any unfair judgment.

The barrister nods along, his impassive expression giving

nothing away as he scans the room. He appears unempathetic to me, and I wonder if his lack of empathy reflects an apparent disparity between his world of privilege and the struggles of the family facing him. It seems Andy is just another case to him, and Shelly and Lenny are just another set of parents navigating the complexities of the criminal justice system. Watching this exchange, I can see that his focus is solely on getting the job done, with no emotional investment. This cold detachment sharply contrasts with Andy's family's raw emotional vulnerability, leaving them feeling frustrated and unheard.

Shelly struggles to follow the barrister's words as he elaborates that Andy is facing a forty-eight-month sentence, which would be reduced due to his guilty plea. After he is finished talking, he leaves them standing there with unanswered questions, trying to understand what they have just been told.

Nervously entering courtroom two at 2 p.m. for Andy's sentencing, Shelly clutches Lenny's hand tightly, while Bella and Aron exchange tense glances, both inhaling deeply to calm their nerves. The smell inside the courtroom is a pungent and peculiar mix of stale coffee and fresh paint. The room is square-shaped, with rows of seats on either side. In the centre, are two desks facing the judge – one for the prosecution and one for the defence barristers. A raised platform at the front houses the judge's bench, and just below it is a space reserved for the court clerk and usher. To my left, a large screen looms, sparking my curiosity. I wonder if it's intended for Andy's appearance via video link from prison.

'All rise,' the command echoes as the judge enters. The room instantly falls into a profound silence. Amid this eerie quiet, Bella's muffled sobs are the only sound.

Andy's image appears on the screen. Dressed in a drab

prison tracksuit, he appears noticeably thinner than before and looks scared and distracted. His voice breaks as he confirms his identity. The court session begins with the prosecution barrister delivering a compelling summary of the evidence against Andy. Everyone in the courtroom listens intently as the prosecuting barrister vividly lays out the extensive list of incriminating evidence. Lenny is alert and attentive, while Shelly sits quietly, her hands clasped in her lap, tears streaming silently down her face. Meanwhile, as Shelly and Bella weep, I notice a man in a black Levi's T-shirt and casual jeans, staring intensely at them. It crosses my mind that he might be the undercover police officer who had apprehended Andy, the key witness in the case. It surprised me that Andy hadn't sensed his presence when the man posed as a drug user. Police officers often have a distinct demeanour one that is hard to explain, but can best be described as a stiffness or rigidity that sets them apart from the public. The man's gaze remains fixed on the family as the barrister outlines the mitigating circumstances.

Andy's defence barrister carefully presents the mitigating factors that could influence the court in reducing his sentence. He emphasizes that this is Andy's first offence and points to the glowing character references from his football coach, former schoolteacher and Bella. They all speak to Andy's kindness and dedication. Bella's reference, which I saw her spend days drafting, paints a picture of how loving he is and how deeply he cares for his mother when her depression spikes. Bella's reference portrays Andy as remorseful, indicating that his actions are an isolated incident that will not be repeated.

We all sit silently, waiting as the judge prepares to announce Andy's sentence. Looking at Andy on the screen, I see the fear and anxiety in his eyes as he awaits his fate. The judge's words begin to blur, but his compassionate tone resonates deeply with all of us. He acknowledges Andy's age, just eighteen, that this was his first offence, that he has a robust support system and that the character references submitted on his behalf paint a very different picture from the one in the case file.

The judge's careful words bring a quiet sense of relief, a feeling that Andy's positive character is finally being recognized. When the verdict is finally delivered, Andy is sentenced to twelve months in prison, reduced from forty-eight months because of his early guilty plea and other mitigating circumstances.

Andy will serve time for supplying Class A drugs. It is still a prison sentence, still time lost, but, for once, it feels as if the system has seen beyond the offence. It has seen the person behind it, a young man who made a mistake – not a gang member or hardened criminal – someone who still has a future. The emotional release ripples through all of us.

Bella breaks down in tears. Lenny, who never cries and is usually stoic, shows his vulnerability by crying too, and even Aron, generally reserved, bows his head in silent thanks. Despite the severity of the situation, there is a feeling of peace and gratitude as we leave courtroom two, knowing the outcome could have been so much worse.

Shelley wastes no time updating Andy's grandparents about his sentence, while Lenny expresses his gratitude to the defence barrister. As we prepare to leave the magistrate's court, the man I suspect to be an undercover officer is eyeing us. He approaches Lenny and Shelly, who register his presence and brace themselves for more incriminating words about their son. But what he says next surprises us all.

The officer reveals that Andy changed his view of young boys involved in drug dealing. He was struck by Andy's behaviour – how he treated him with kindness, engaged him in conversation and even shared a laugh. The officer noted that this was a stark contrast to how other drug dealers under surveillance treated him. He expressed satisfaction with Andy receiving a reduced sentence and mentioned he would share his compassionate perspective with his superiors, hoping it might encourage a more open-minded approach to police work in the future.

Shelly listens patiently, but her scepticism is clear, and understandably so. Her weariness is rooted in a long, troubling history of racially biased policing in England, a history that continues to shape the experiences of Black communities today. The 1970s and 1980s were particularly noteworthy periods, when moral panics about 'black muggings'[1] and the Brixton uprisings[2] contributed to an atmosphere of fear and suspicion, severely straining the relationship between the police and communities of colour. During this time, the controversial 'sus law'[3], which effectively allowed police to stop and search young Black men under dubious pretences, became emblematic of a heavy-handed and discriminatory approach to policing. These tactics deepened mistrust and resentment, leaving lasting scars on the Black communities' relationship with the police. Lord Scarman's investigation into the 1980s uprisings[4] acknowledged the presence of discriminatory policing practices, and this troubling legacy was further brought to light in 1993, following the racially motivated murder of teenager Stephen Lawrence. This case shocked the nation and provoked widespread mourning. In response, the Macpherson Report[5] was published, categorically identifying the Metropolitan Police as institutionally racist, and exposing the ongoing impact of racism within British policing.

As we entered the new millennium, conversations about race and policing continued to evolve. The David Lammy Review[6] exposed the deep-rooted racial bias embedded in the UK's criminal justice system. Fast forward to 2023 when the Baroness Casey Review[7] reiterated the urgent need for reform, presenting further evidence of racism within the police force. Despite the clear findings, a pressing question remains: What, if anything, has fundamentally changed in the policing of Black men?

What becomes painfully clear is that the legacy of oppressive policing in Black communities cannot be understood in isolation; rather it is intricately linked to a broader historical continuum shaped by slavery and colonialism and systemic inequality. These forces are not confined to the past – they have evolved over time, embedding themselves in contemporary policing and law and order. Over the decades, this ongoing impact has been documented repeatedly, with numerous studies and official statistics – including reports from the Home Office – highlighting the issue of persistent racial profiling and systemic discrimination. Individuals from Black, Asian and minority ethnic backgrounds often face disproportionately harsh consequences due to policing practices, experiencing greater scrutiny than their white counterparts. This is particularly evident in the high rates of stop-and-search incidents targeting Black boys and men and reinforces a reality in which, for many, interactions with the police are clouded by police officers' unwarranted suspicion and surveillance of young Black men. These enduring dynamics only deepen tension between police and the very communities they are meant to serve and protect.

As the police officer walks away, Shelly turns to us, scepticism heavy in her voice. 'Nothing will change,' she says, drawing on her personal pain and the long history shared by many around her.

Lenny, who feels more sympathy for the officer, offers a gentler perspective. 'Love, he was just doing his job. Andy wouldn't be in this position if he hadn't sold drugs.'

Shelly's reply is sharp and unyielding. 'Well, they've got him now. They've always targeted and harassed our son.' Her words are heavy, and I can feel the weight of her truth.

Andy and his friends have had numerous encounters with the police over the years, even before they got involved in life on road. It troubles me to recall that some of their earliest run-ins happened when they were barely teenagers. I remember the day he and Aron were innocently enjoying their summer holidays, walking back from the Grove Youth Club, when officers descended upon them, suspecting them of involvement in a nearby robbery simply because they matched a questionable description. Then there was Cassius, whose story was no different: he was arrested and charged for a similar offence – one that he vehemently denies committing, his voice disregarded by a system all too eager to label him.

It was clear that, although Andy had crossed a line this time, a few kind words from a reflective police officer would do little to restore Shelly's shattered trust in a police force she believed consistently targeted her son and others like him. The boys were far too often branded as 'usual suspects', and the scars from their encounters ran deep.

We arrive back at Andy's house in the early evening. Everyone is gathered to hear the outcome of Andy's court hearing. Cassius didn't attend court, but has arrived now, hoping to keep a low profile and avoid Shelly, just in case the court case didn't go well. Zak is here too, sizing up to Aron, with a tense, troubled expression. He looks visibly upset, on the edge of losing his composure.

'If you do the crime, you do the time,' Zak shouts at Aron with reckless bravado.

'What's wrong with you, blud? Do you think Auntie Shelly needs you out here running your mouth?' Aron snaps back, moving closer to his brother with his fist clenched.

Zak isn't reading the room and repeats, 'If you do the crime, you do the time.'

Cassius swiftly intervenes in the brewing conflict, positioning himself between the two to prevent a physical altercation.

Aron's voice rises in agitation. 'Not everyone can find a job as easily as you. You don't have a clue what a man is going through.' He wrestles against Cassius's attempts to hold him back, his anger growing. 'You grew up in a different era, bruv,' he yells as Cassius tries to push him away from Zak.

Zak slurs his words, and replies, 'You can't be on the roads forever. One day, the fuckery you do on road will catch up to you. I was able to leave it behind – why can't you?'

Zak's words and hostility catch me off guard, especially considering his past. There was a time when he, too, was on the roads, fully aware of the challenges accompanying the lifestyle. But Aron is right: they did grow up in different times and walked similar, yet different, paths. While Zak dabbled in the illegal drug trade during his youth, he consistently managed to hold down a job, mainly in retail, and was not involved in the postcode wars that trap his younger brother. The rivalries between estates were common in the late 1980s when Zak was in his teens, but those conflicts were fought with fists, unlike the lethal weapons that define the struggles of Aron's generation in Northville.

Though Zak gained some recognition in his circles, he never attained the kind of infamous notoriety that now clings to his brother like a permanent stain, colouring every aspect of Aron's existence. In contrast, having transitioned out of the lifestyle, Zak now carries himself with an air of authority, though it's clear he hasn't fully grasped the complexities of his younger brother's reality.

As the argument intensifies, I can sense the growing emotional distance between the brothers. Aron struggles against that same tide, unable to carve out a more stable trajectory like Zak has, highlighting how their lives have evolved into entirely separate worlds.

Still furious, Aron's voice is thick with emotion as he says, 'You weren't on the roads like we are. You can be a normal civilian. When have you been a big brother to me? When man violated me, you didn't do shit. I'm my [own] big brother; I'm outside alone!'

Before Zak can respond, Shelly emerges from the house, demanding an end to the escalating conflict. 'I've lost my son. I don't need you two making matters worse. We're family; we have to stick together,' she says, bringing Aron and Zak face to face, their expressions mirroring the pain and regret swirling between them.

Her intervention helps diffuse the tension, and Zak and Aron agree to have a heart-to-heart the following day.

Shelly sensed how fragile their relationship had become, strained under the weight of unresolved grievances, and she was determined to mend the growing rift within her family. Her plea struck a chord with her nephews, especially as they prepared for the emotional challenges that the coming year promised. With significant milestones like Christmas and the impending arrival of Bella's second child on the horizon, the absence of Andy felt heavier than ever, making the need for family even more crucial. They all knew that during this challenging time they needed to stay close – not just as a family but as a source of strength for each other.

It's a cold morning in September, the day Andy comes home. He's being released early on tag, a system used for people serving short sentences.

As we approach the prison, Bella seems restless. She fidgets with the windows in the car, rolling them up and down, annoying Cassius.

'Bella, relax, man,' he says. 'He's coming home; why are you moving mad?'

'I'm happy. I just don't know how he'll be since he stopped calling us,' she expresses.

Cassius responds, 'You're always taking things so personally, but that's what we do – we ride the bird alone sometimes. It's easier for us. Sometimes, speaking to family reminds man of home too much and makes the time inside proper hard,' Cassius explains, drawing from his experience of spending much of his teenage years in and out of prison and understanding the challenges of adapting to life inside.

'I didn't talk to my mum for at least six months when I got the longest bird,' he continues.

'How did you manage alone for so long?' I ask him.

'It's minor. When you're in and out of prison, you get used to it and adapt to your new surroundings, he explains. 'My mum would have just made my time in there more stressful;

she's always fussing and worrying too much. I didn't wanna add to her stress telling her how rough it really was.'

'Was it hard for you?' I probe. This is a topic Cassius rarely discusses.

'Yes, of course it was hard. It's not a bed of roses,' he admits. 'You're not free. You're restricted. You're sharing your cell with a stranger, and I've had some strange ones, I tell you that much.'

'What do you mean by strange?' I ask.

With a sigh, he recounts, 'I've had a cellmate who was really struggling. He used to randomly start shouting in the middle of the night, waking man up every second. He was always high on spice; nuff man in there were high on some drug. I didn't get no proper sleep in there. I had to keep one eye open. It was a madness.'

He shakes his head, the memories flooding back. 'It's just a place of filth. It stinks. It's dirty. You got man wiping their arse in front of you – there's no privacy. The food is minging. Luckily, I had family to send me money, so I was eating good and had the essentials. But there are some men in there that don't have family support, so they do what they need to do to survive. Prison has the same politics as the roads, man.'

He continues, 'Imagine being banged up with all these men. Most have something to prove; you don't know if you should look left or right. The politics you go through on road follows you in there too. You still have to watch your back, and man expects you to ride for the endz if something goes down.'

Bella interjects, 'Yeah, I remember Andy talking about something like that during one of our phone calls a couple of months back. I got worried when I heard that and wanted him home more than ever.'

Cassius nods. 'It's deep, man. I remember one of the mandem from the endz got in a fight with a man from a different part of town,' he recalls, his voice becoming more serious. 'I didn't jump in, and the news flew around the outside world. I know Ash and Aron got into it with a yout from Northville who was trying disrespect me to other mandem.'

As we get closer to the prison gates, Cassius's tone shifts, revealing a mix of relief and awareness. 'I'm glad Andy made it through with his mind intact. It's a mad ting, prison life. I ain't trying to go back there.'

After waiting outside for around ten minutes, the sturdy grey metal doors finally groan open, and Andy steps out into the daylight. It's an emotional whirlwind: Bella wraps him in a tearful embrace, while Aron sprays him with champagne. Yet Andy's expression remains distant, as if lost in thought, taking in the world beyond the prison walls for the first time in what must have felt like an eternity.

Bella bombards her brother with questions as we drive home, but he barely responds and stares out of the window, more interested in the passing scenery outside. He quietly requests Aron to stop at McDonald's before heading home, and after two hours we're back in Northville.

Shelly is already waiting outside with Lenny. When she spots Cassius's car, she sprints towards it. 'Praise the Lord, my son, my son is home,' she cries as she and Lenny embrace Andy. For the first time, as his mother and father hold him, Andy can truly relax. He then rushes past the crowd of friends gathered outside, spudding those he can as he hurries into the house. He seems more focused on getting inside than on anything else. Bella looks worried as she turns to Aron, asking if he thinks Andy is doing okay. Aron takes her hand gently and reassures her that they shouldn't overwhelm him; he'll need some time to settle in.

Inside the house, Andy's welcome-home party is in full swing. The music is loud, dominoes clack against the table, and quiet laughter rises around us. But Andy sits quietly, a little removed from it all, fidgeting with his lighter. I can only imagine it all feels too loud, too fast – almost unreal. It's a lot to take in.

Shelly rushes over, balancing a plate piled high with Andy's favourites: rice and peas, fried chicken, plantain and homemade coleslaw – all the comfort of home packed in one meal.

'I've really missed your food, Mum,' Andy murmurs, a gentle smile on his face as he takes the plate. Shelly's face lights up, as if she's been waiting to hear those words for a long time.

Cassius leans in and hands Andy his first spliff, quietly asking why he ignored some of the mandem outside. Andy exhales slowly, his eyes drifting to Aron. 'Only you and Aron sent me any Ps when I was in there,' he says. 'Half the mandem didn't even answer my calls.' He doesn't name names – he doesn't have to. I saw the ones he blanked on his way inside.

Cassius nods in agreement. 'Same ting happened to me. You find out quick who your real dawgs are when you're locked down.'

Andy shakes his head in disbelief. 'Man called Jake [another friend] for £50. Told me to hit him up tomorrow. I did – he aired me. Now he's outside bussing champs like he's my day one.' His jaw tightens. 'I needed help. Not his fake love.'

His voice lowers, but the anger's still there. 'I'm about to tell them all to move from the door. I just wanna be with fam. Family first.'

Cassius stands up and gives him a fist bump. 'Family first. I got you.' Then he heads towards the front door to tell some of the mandem to go home – he knows exactly who they are.

Andy watches him leave, his shoulders relaxing just a little. He's finally starting to feel at ease, and the look in his eyes reveals everything; he's done begging for loyalty that should've always been there.

Several weeks pass before I run into Andy again, this time at a community event in Grove Park, on a windy afternoon. He's surrounded by his family, but even in their company he looks as if he is miles away, fidgeting with the keys in his hand, as if the happiness around him is out of his reach.

When I ask how life has been since he got out of prison, he gives a half-smile and says, 'I can't complain. It feels good to be home.' But something about his expression feels off; he looks restless, uncertain.

He mentions that he's applied for an apprenticeship, but weeks have passed with no news. There's also a warehouse job he's considering, and he's thinking about getting a CSCS card like his godbrother, who's managed to find work on a building site, even with a criminal record.

'That's such good news,' I say, smiling, trying to stay upbeat even though I'm worried. It's encouraging to hear about his efforts to build a new path after prison – especially given the disheartening statistics from Public Health England (2021)[8], which highlight staggering reoffending rates among 18–25-year-olds. Unfortunately, Andy fell right into that demographic.

'I'm really trying man,' he says, the tiredness in his voice clear. 'But if they don't get back to me soon, I'm just gonna give up. I don't care any more.'

He shrugs off the idea of calling to follow up on his application. 'I'm not running people down,' he mutters, which feels more like self-protection than pride. He admits he didn't finish school and fears that employers want more than he can offer. Then in a softer voice he adds, 'I don't know how to fit into that world. I can't handle it.'

Before I can say anything, Bella shows up with her newborn baby, Trey, short for Treysharn, and Andy walks off to join the mandem for a football game. I stay with Bella on the grass, and soon her concerns come through.

Bella says Andy hasn't found any of the jobs he keeps talking about – it's actually been her doing the searching. During the day, he doesn't do much of anything, and he's out late most nights. She's worried he might be back to selling, even though he insists he's just depressed and finding things hard.

'He was dealing for over two years, and none of us knew,' she says. 'Now I'm just waiting for the next shock to hit the family.'

Despite her worries, she still wants to believe in him. She's wishing he'll get the apprenticeship, that he'll come off the roads for good – but there's hesitation in her voice.

'I want to trust him,' she says quietly. 'I really do. But I don't know if I can.'

And I can hear the confusion – that quiet pain of someone who's been let down too many times, yet still clings to hope.

I leave Bella alone with her swirling thoughts, a heavy sadness settling over me for their family. You'd think that

Andy's return would lift some of the weight from their shoulders, but I am beginning to realize that a different set of challenges looms on the horizon.

The truth is that Bella and her family can't predict what lies ahead for Andy. Will the apprenticeship for which he hopes come through? Will other job opportunities appear? The most unsettling question, however, lingers at the back of my mind: will he have the strength to take those opportunities if they do?

I can see how much stress this uncertainty is causing Bella. She looks like a tightly wound spring, filled with worry about her brother's future. Bella is doing her best to hold things together, working alongside Shelly. Together, they pour all their love and energy into supporting him after prison – but the challenges just keep coming.

Andy has stepped back into the familiar neighbourhood, but nothing has really changed. The same temptations are still there, ready to pull him back into old habits. When we talked quietly, he admitted it was getting harder to resist the roads – that struggle was always there, lurking just beneath the surface of his thoughts.

Change, I realized, wouldn't come quickly. It would be a slow, tough fight against the pull of a life that still felt so familiar. Only time will tell if he can take the big step into mainstream, supported by a family that desperately wants to see him thrive and overcome the daunting odds stacked before him: the fear of becoming someone different and daring to dream beyond the tight grip of the roads.

CHAPTER 7

Shebeen

I'm sitting in the dimly lit shebeen, located at the back of Mr T's grocery store, affectionately called Tionne's, after its owner. Somehow, its lively presence had escaped my notice until now. In the day, you wouldn't know that the shebeen existed – it's a fully stocked grocery store, selling the freshest yams, green bananas and plantain. But, as night falls, Mr T's store transforms into a vibrant social hub. This particular evening, the community elders gather to engage in the age-old traditions of dominoes and Ludi. Their joyous laughter and animated conversations echo through the small square space as they sway to Sizzla's 'One Away' playing from the modest sound system. The handcrafted speakers, power amplifiers and vintage turntable deliver soul-stirring melodies that transport you to another world. There's food here too; someone is cooking curry chicken, which mixes with the smell of rum, making it familiar and calm.

Mr T notices the anxiety that I can't quite conceal, and I fidget nervously, acutely aware of the unfamiliar faces surrounding me. With a warm smile, he approaches and hands me a perfectly mixed rum and Coke. What strikes me most about Mr T is his warm aura and his uncanny resemblance to my late grandfather. He has the same smooth, dark skin untouched by the passage of time, a strong and dignified stature and expressive eyes that seem to hold a universe of stories. Both men hailed from Jamaica, and their thick patois accents remained unchanged despite the years they've spent in England. They brought with them a wealth of experiences from a bygone era vastly different from mine. Their migration from Jamaica to England in search of better opportunities paints a vivid picture in my thoughts of the courage it must have taken to leave everything familiar behind to pursue a brighter future.

In an instant, I feel a bond with Mr T, as if I have found a piece of my own heritage here. The initial nervousness melts away as I revel in our comforting familiarity. Mr T settles into a sturdy wooden chair, and I express my eagerness to find out what the elder generation thinks about the violence in Northville. His response is encouraging. His eyes gleam with the wisdom of a life well lived as he starts recounting his story.

'I came to England before you were born, in the 1960s, to join my uncle who had already settled here,' he says, pointing to a black-and-white framed photograph above the sound system. The image shows a striking young gentleman, elegantly dressed in a sleek, well-tailored suit, meticulously groomed, exuding the refined sophistication characteristic of that era.

'That's my uncle Harold,' he says, his voice filled with affection. 'He came to England in the 1940s looking for work and sent for me.'

He pauses for a moment, looking thoughtful. 'I didn't want to leave Jamaica – it's my home. But my late mother wanted me to emigrate to England for better opportunities.'

A small sigh comes from him. 'It was hard to adjust to the new culture.' Then a sense of pride shines through his voice.

'But I'm grateful I came. I made a fulfilling life for myself, gave my kids and grandkids a better start in life.' A smile spreads across his face, genuine and full, as if he feels content with this journey.

Mr T's migration story echoes the dreams and determination of many Caribbean migrants who came to the UK searching for new opportunities. He followed family members who had already made the journey, with some arriving as far back as 1948 on the *Empire Windrush* – the ship that symbolized the beginning of large-scale Caribbean emigration to Britain. When he arrived, he and his late uncle devoted themselves to establishing a life in their new homeland. Opening their beloved grocery shop, Tionne's, in the 1970s, it quickly became one of the most popular stores in the bustling heart of London's vibrant Caribbean community in Northville. The shebeen at the back played a crucial role in uniting the Caribbean community.

Shebeens have long been a vital part of Caribbean culture, serving as important social hubs for migrants who often faced exclusion from traditional leisure venues, like pubs and nightclubs. In an environment marked by discrimination, these establishments provided a much-needed refuge, allowing the Caribbean community to come together, revel in a taste of home, celebrate their heritage and express themselves freely, away from the constraints of prejudice. Being at Tionne's reminds me of the sense of community I felt at the shubs I attended a few months ago – both spaces embody a spirit of ownership and togetherness, fostering a shared sense of belonging among those who gather there.

Immersed in Tionne's heart-warming atmosphere, it becomes evident why places like these have withstood the test of time. Here the elders swap stories, reminisce about their homelands and discuss the challenges of modern life in an era defined by hardship, and thus shebeens not only preserve cultural traditions and foster a strong sense of community but also provide moments of joy and a brief respite from the harsh realities of life in a working-class neighbourhood. They serve as a source of camaraderie in the face of adversity, continuing to be a beacon of hope and resilience.

'Work was hard today. I wanna give up this night job, but Sheila will kill me,' I overhear an elder say before he smashes a domino piece on the table in frustration and takes a sip from his bottle of Guinness.

In response, another elder chimes in, 'Working in this Babylon system is tough, Jah know. We're all struggling, but Jah tell us we have to survive; we have to persevere the forces of oppression,' he says, taking a drag from his spliff.

Meanwhile, a different elder admits to selling 'sensi', a term for cannabis, to cope with the rising cost of living in the city. This admission highlights a harsh reality faced by a group of elderly men from various social backgrounds in Northville. Among them are low-wage workers and those caught in poverty and unemployment, reflecting the deepening inequality that has overtaken the UK, particularly in its most impoverished inner-city neighbourhoods like Northville.

Since the devastating financial crisis of 2008[1], those already enduring poverty have faced increasing hardships. The austerity measures implemented by the Conservative–Liberal Democrat coalition government in 2010 only worsened the situation for the most vulnerable groups. Among those most affected by the welfare changes are elderly community members who struggle to find employment, many of whom have fallen into extreme poverty. For the elderly men gathered in the shebeen this evening, it is not just a place to relax amid their challenging circumstances. Here, surrounded by the scent of rum and shared stories, they have found a much-needed respite from their daily struggles. They forge connections that remind them of their shared humanity in a world that often overlooks people in their age group.

Not long after 9 p.m. two women rush into Tionne's, carrying bulky rucksacks, with sleeping bags sticking out, scanning the room looking for a man named Bentley. The younger of the two women sits across from me, her eyes fixed on the scuffed floorboards. She looks oddly familiar, and when she finally looks up I catch a glimpse of her former self. Though her beauty and radiant smile have faded, the sparkle in her emerald eyes has gone and her appearance is dishevelled, I recognize Abby, a childhood friend from my primary-school days.

Memories flood back of our walks home together, the shared laughter as we swung high on the swings at the park and the moments spent at Vinnie's enjoying her favourite bubble-gum ice lolly. After primary school, we lost touch, but I recalled seeing her as a lively teenager at a local fun fair once. Now, she is barely recognizable.

'Abby,' I say. I can sense her trying to place me as our eyes meet.

'Wow . . . Oh my God, Ebony, is that you?' She comes towards me and gives me a tight hug.

'How have you been?' I enquire, although I can see that her life has taken a turn.

'I can't complain, you know. I'm still breathing,' Abby replies, absentmindedly scratching her left arm, her struggle with drug addiction transparent in her demeanour. 'It's been rough over the last few years,' she continues. 'I lost my mum in 2010, and life has never been the same since.'

At this moment, I sit with her, holding space for her, like I did as a kid. Her voice quivers with vulnerability as she confides in me about the challenges she's faced since her mother passed away – a loss that spiralled her into a world of substance abuse. Abby's mother battled with her own addiction to alcohol, and Abby was often her caregiver. After she passed, she went to live with her aunt, who also struggled in life. Seeking comfort and support, she found solace with an older man in the community known for his drug abuse and sexual predation. He got her hooked on drugs and took away her self-esteem and agency. Now, Abby is living on the streets and struggling to survive. Without a stable home, she has found it extremely challenging to find employment and to access the necessary social services to help her get back on her feet.

When I look into her eyes, I feel a deep sadness. They seem empty – a reminder of the struggles so many face when addiction takes hold. The painful stigma around drug use is brutal; it pushes people to the sidelines, rendering them outcasts, who lose the empathy and respect they so desperately need. As Canadian physician and trauma specialist Gabor Maté famously stated, 'Addiction is not a choice that anybody makes; it's not a moral failure; it's not an ethical lapse; it's not a weakness of character; it's not a failure of will . . .'[2] Society often oversimplifies the struggles of those grappling with substance abuse, perceiving them as having voluntarily chosen a path of self-destruction. This mindset obscures the complex and often heartbreaking stories behind their compulsive behaviour – stories like Abby's, filled with trauma, loss and the relentless pursuit of relief from their pain.

'I just can't get back to being me,' she confesses, her voice breaking. 'Every day I wake up telling myself I'm gonna change, but when I find myself on the streets getting clean feels impossible.'

I gently enquire about her cousins, recalling the closeness they once shared. 'What happened? Can they not help you?'

'You might as well say they've disowned me – they think I'm gonna steal from them. They don't trust me,' she admits. 'They used to invite me into their homes and watch me like I'm some criminal, so worried about their expensive sofas getting dirty. They wouldn't even let me sit on their chairs, let alone sleep in their beds.' The realization that she is utterly alone hangs heavy in her voice, each word soaked in the sorrow of abandonment.

'I'm so sorry,' are the only words I can manage, as I feel overwhelmed by the tragedy of her situation. Her cousins, who were once a source of support, have now turned against her, cruelly branding her a thief and shunning her desperate cries for help. The pain in her voice leaves me at a loss for how to respond, so I simply listen.

'I'm invisible to them, to everyone really. They think I must want to be like this,' she adds. 'Even when I'm high, I would never dream of robbing my family or anyone. I just feel trapped in a nightmare. I can't manage my thoughts, the grief, the pain; doing drugs stops it all.'

In that moment, I see a glimpse of the Abby I once knew – a bright, self-aware girl hidden beneath the heavy layers of addiction. Her clarity is gut-wrenching; she understands her inner turmoil and the reasons driving her dependency, revealing a faint spark of her resilient spirit trapped inside, but is powerless to break free.

'I don't wanna work the streets for money,' she continues, her gaze drifting away from mine. 'But this is me for now; I'm doing whatever I can to survive. It won't be forever.'

As she shares her story with me, there is a subtle wariness in her eyes, almost as if she is questioning whether I, too, am judging her. I can feel the weight of shame in her words, a shame that only serves to perpetuate the tragic cycle of addiction she yearns to escape.

As we sit in Tionne's, surrounded by the lively chatter and laughter of the elders, we catch up and reminisce about our childhood together. She laughs, only for it to turn into tears as she recalls visiting Tionne's when Valery was alive. Mr T and Valery were kindred spirits, connected by their love of music and cooking. Tionne's had become a second home to Abby, and as I watch him bring her bottles of water and sandwiches it becomes clear just how much of a lifeline he is for her, especially in her darkest hours. Like the community of elders that gathers here, Tionne's has also become a refuge for Abby, offering solace in times of need. Mr T's unwavering support and empathy stand as a reassuring presence in her life. It is hard to imagine where she would be without his kindness, especially in a world that often lacks compassion.

'Abby, take these and stay out of trouble – you hear me? Make sure you come back tomorrow. I'm making some gungo peas soup.' He carefully tucks the food and drinks into her rucksack.

'Thank you, Uncle. You know I love me some gungo peas soup. You make it just like Mummy. I'll come check you in the evening.' With these parting words, Abby disappears into the night with Bentley, a well-known local drug dealer. I never see her again after our reunion at Tionne's.

Two elders take their place beside me. Their curious eyes lock on to mine as one leans in to ask for my name, clearly surprised by the appearance of a new face among them. They – Rudy and Clive – listen intently as I introduce myself and explain why I'm here.

Clive is a retired Jamaican gentleman. He radiates an air of elegance, wearing a sharp suit and a timeless bowler hat that hides his short plaits underneath. Clive has lived in England since the age of thirteen, which adds up to forty-three years in the country. He proudly reminisces about his time working as a security officer and his six-year tenure in the army. He highlights his strong work ethic and the satisfaction of earning a decent living for most of his life. But two years ago, he faced redundancy, and since then, he's been trying to break free from the monotony of unemployment by frequently visiting Tionne's.

In contrast, Rudy, is a retired musician in his sixties, with a subtle yet powerful authority. He has resided in England for forty-nine years, going to school here, working various jobs, including positions at a pharmacy and a hospital, before pursuing his passion for music. He is preparing to perform one of his songs tonight.

Rudy takes over the conversation when I ask him what it's like to live in Northville. His eyebrows raise, and he taps his Clarks boots on the floor, eager to share his worries.

'These young ones have made the area a dangerous place to live in.' He pauses, shaking his head slowly. 'All this killing one another – it's no good.'

Leaning forward, he puts his fingers together. 'I would tell them, listen to your mum and dad. You must honour your mother and father. You must obey.'

For a moment, Rudy looks up, as if remembering an old lesson. 'It is vanity. This younger generation deal with vanity. They put these things before themselves.'

He exhales heavily, his voice strong yet tired. 'You have to put Jah ahead of everything.'

Rudy is a passionate follower of His Imperial Majesty Emperor Haile Selassie I[3], firmly believing in peace, love, self-improvement, and gaining knowledge. He feels that today's younger generation has become disconnected from themselves, becoming preoccupied with the shallow and materialistic aspects of the modern world. He says many young people lack guidance and associate with 'bad company', engaging in behaviours that contradict his values.

As mentioned earlier, it's common for the mandem to turn to Islam for spiritual enlightenment and guidance to make sense of their experiences, but in the 1970s many Black men from lower class backgrounds, facing discrimination and racism, turned to Rastafari[4] for solace and understanding. Rudy arrived in England during the racially charged 1960s, and it's easy to imagine the deep insecurity that enveloped the Black community during that time. Individuals like Rudy sought refuge in Rastafarianism to cope with the racism and oppression they encountered and to uplift their sense of self. While Rudy is not embittered by his life experiences, there's a noticeable undertone of frustration and perhaps even anger in his feelings towards the younger generation, as he perceives that they are not striving to lead righteous lives and elevate themselves.

Amid the lively chatter and the clinking of rum glasses, Rudy and Clive passionately discuss their strict upbringing in Jamaica. They express concerns about how cultural values seem to have faded among today's youth and blame a lack of discipline for rising crime and violence in the community.

Rudy leans in, filled with emotion, as he shares his story. 'I was brought up by my grandparents back home,' he begins. 'When they died, that's when my parents send for me to dwell with them in this country.' He pauses for a moment, as if remembering an important lesson his grandparents taught him about the value of discipline.

He shakes his head slowly, recalling the differences. 'The culture's gone through the window. In my day, I couldn't tell Mum and Dad to eff off! Me dead. That couldn't run.'

For Rudy, the problem seems to stem from shifting power dynamics. 'Since Thatcher ruled out the discipline, everything went sky high. Children think they have power over you. You can't even rough them up.' He gestures with his hand in the air, illustrating a small tree. 'You have to bend the tree when it's small. Once it gets big, it's too late.'

Beside him, Clive nods in agreement. 'Exactly. When my son was younger, he got into so much trouble with the police.' He sighs. 'I hit him, but you know the first thing he said to me? Dad, I know the number for Childline. That's when I realized – I couldn't hit him again, so I hand him over to the government.'

He raises his drink and takes a slow sip, before speaking in a softer tone. 'My father was a police officer in Jamaica. Man was strict. But my son?' He shakes his head. 'He always been unruly. Never wanted to listen. Even try fight me as he got older.'

As I listen intently to Rudy and Clive exchange their rich stories for hours, I can almost picture their world – an England marked by riots, sus laws, deep-rooted discrimination, pervasive prejudice and economic recession. Rudy describes this world as 'Babylon holding people down'. However, despite these challenges, I sense a spirit of optimism and a desire to carve a path into the mainstream, regardless of the adversity surrounding them.

I begin reflecting on the differences between the generations Clive and Rudy describe. Is there a distinction? It is clear that Clive and Rudy demonstrated great resilience; they own their homes, held mainstream jobs and raised families while pushing back against systemic oppression. Yet I see that the systems they battled against have not changed much for the younger generation. This shared struggle connects both generations, despite their apparent differences in goals and achievements.

What really strikes me is that, while Clive and Rudy had made it through to adulthood – juggling work and family – the mandem seem stuck. They feel cut off from society, trapped on the roads. This reminded me of Victor Turner's 1969 idea of 'liminal space'[5], a stage where someone is caught between phases – set apart from society, almost invisible, stuck in transition.[6] In a similar way, the mandem find themselves in this in-between space; the roads reflect this vulnerable position where they are left in limbo, trapped in their neighbourhoods, caught up in the drug trade – a mindset from which it is difficult to break free – and they don't quite make it into successful adulthood. Ultimately, this holds them back from reaching their full potential.

I find it interesting that Clive and Rudy do not talk directly about the roads, but I'm starting to see how their experiences as fathers show their struggles with the lifestyle, and they both acknowledge the issues within the community.

It is clear that for a different generation road life did not carry the same significance, although I'm convinced that the lifestyle existed during their time, albeit expressed differently. After all, youth-street cultures typically emerge as reflections of broader societal conditions – conditions that both Clive and Rudy lived through and with which they are deeply familiar.

Road life, street life and the emergence of subcultures are not new phenomena; they have been present in society for decades, extending beyond the UK. Take, for instance, the rude boys, who emerged in post-war Jamaica – the homeland of both Clive and Rudy. I couldn't help but feel that they were well acquainted with this subculture, especially since my father, a fellow Kingstonian, often shared stories with me about their origins. He vividly described how, in the shadows of Kingston's impoverished shantytowns after the country's independence in 1962, young men emerged, inspired by characters from gangster and cowboy films. These rude boys arose in response to the dire social and economic conditions of that era, which was marked by widespread poverty, soaring unemployment, political unrest and pervasive gang violence.

Their story became the focal point of countless reggae songs, one of the most iconic being The Slickers' 1970s hit 'Johnny Too Bad'[7], featured on the soundtrack of the legendary film *The Harder They Come*[8], which personified the spirit of the Kingston rude boy and highlighted the plight of marginalized and disenfranchised youth throughout Jamaica. As the rude-boy subculture made its way to Britain during the second wave of immigration, it transformed into a profound symbol within Black British culture and music, representing the hardships of poverty and marginalization while simultaneously embodying the archetypical 'bad boy' persona that captured the imagination of many.

Given their sons' involvement in this world and the rich history of subcultures – especially the rude boys – I decided to be more direct with my question. So, eager to delve deeper into their insights on road life, I ask Clive and Rudy, 'What is road culture?'

Rudy is the first to respond. His voice is steady, but there is a hint of concern. 'Not knowing where you are going,' he reflects for a moment, then continues, 'What we built in the early days, the younger generation do not carry it on. They turn to wickedness.'

Clive chimes in, 'It's an eediat ting,' waving his hand in the air.

Rudy looks at Clive, and they share a knowing nod.

Rudy goes on, 'What my ancestors been through during slavery, our age group tried to make things better.' He takes a deep breath, as if trying to push the memory away. 'We didn't want our children to go through that. That's why many of us leave the West Indian islands, come over here, so our kids could get a better life.' He taps his chest, speaking with passion.

'After we slave and go through all of that, we try to set an example for our children to follow. But they do not follow.' A look of disappointment appears on his face. 'They are not honest or faithful to their friend. They backbite their friend.' He raises his hand, palm facing up, as if asking for understanding. 'You need to culture your friend. Pull up your friend.'

Clive nods and replies sincerely, 'We don't come from a culture like that, not violence like this. We try to make peace. We are the same; we are one.'

Rudy shakes his head firmly. 'Road culture to me is

rubbish. It is devil business. This road chat about we're bad – it's rubbish: young bwoy dem ah pierce dem ears and pierce their nose, and these young gal ah put stud in dem tongue and in their belly. If you read Isaiah and Jeremiah it will tell you these things. Our great father denounce.'

Curious, I ask, 'What about the men your age who stand outside the bookie shop all day? Would you describe them as road men?'

Rudy's face tightens with disappointment as he talks about these older men – what he calls 'bad sheep'.

'They don't set no example,' he says, his forehead creased in concern.

He leans in, his voice calm but weighed down by memories. 'In my time, I'd leave a job today, take my lunch break, find another job, then leave the next day. Many of us came here not to stay, but to work hard, save money and go back home.' He sighs. 'But some get caught up in the system. A lot of them live bad life. If you do good, goodness follow you; if you do bad, badness follow you. Jah words.'

Cautiously, I ask if they think the older generation was on a bad path when they made poor choices in their youth.

Rudy leans in bit closer, his face serious, as he tries to make sure I really get what he is saying. 'Yes, the sins of the fathers and mothers travel up upon their children,' he explains. 'Their children will suffer because of what they have done.' His voice drops, reflecting the seriousness of his message. 'There are two roads, bad road and good road. If your aim is college, university, that's good. But if you choose to be a thief, you'll always be in and out of prison.' He takes a moment to see how I'm responding.

I nod, keeping my gaze fixed on him.

'What do you expect your children to do? The same as you, innit?'

Rudy's straightens up in his seat. 'Every girl child looks up to their mother as superior and every boy looks at their father as superior. Watch your father.'

There's a clear sense of pride in voice, paired with strong beliefs. 'All my children are doing something with their lives. If they wasn't, I wouldn't want to know.'

He gestures emphatically, clearly thinking back to his past. 'I put them into education after their mother died. Me never go to prison yet, and the police never have my fingerprints. You have to have a clean record to get these top jobs.'

His eyes sharpen as he continues, and his pride turns into firm principle. 'I show them I never lived that kinda life. If one of them ever stepped out of line, don't look for me to help. I'm the kind of father that would tell the judge to lock him up if he had done something wrong.'

Rudy leans back in his chair. 'Parents aren't supposed to surrender to children. Children are supposed to surrender to parents. Don't let your children wrap you round their little finger. Come out me house if you are a big man or woman.'

His words linger, carrying a conviction not just spoken, but lived. A few people around the table nod in agreement, taking in his truth. I nod slowly too, appreciating his realness.

Then Clive offers his final reflection on the sense of unity he feels at Tionne's. 'The majority of us here are Jamaicans. It is nice to have one tribe to unite. This is the bond between us – you see how peaceful it is. If I am down, he will help me. You have to move loving with people. Love is key.'

As Rudy gets ready for his performance, I take a moment to thank both men for sharing their valuable thoughts with me. Before I wrap up, I ask them one final question about their hopes for the future. Rudy shares that his main focus is on his grandchildren – building them a solid foundation for life. He expresses his worries that the younger generation doesn't fully grasp the dangers around them, but hopes they'll find a better way forward. His final thoughts carry both hope for what lies ahead and concern for the direction in which the younger generation is heading.

When Rudy steps on to the stage, excitement and anticipation ripple through the crowd. The infectious rhythm of the reggae music pulses through the room, drawing everyone to their feet as they begin to sway to the beat. With his long dreadlocks swinging, Rudy skanks joyfully, perfectly in tune with the music. His performance is mesmerizing, and his strong voice delivers a powerful message about peace and unity:

> *Put down the gun, me say to put down the gun.*
> *Put down the gun, me say to put down the gun.*
> *No budda shoot your brother down.*

> Do good, my brothers and sisters, in this time.
> Hear what Jah says, do good in your neighbourhood,
>   hear what Jah says.
> Don't smoke no cocaine to mash up your brain.
> We spent too much time in shackles and chains.

> *Put down the gun, me say to put down the gun.*
> *Put down the gun, me say to put down the gun.*
> *No budda shoot your brother down.*

One day, we will be free from all this pain and brutality.
We'll be free from Babylon; we'll be free from Babylon.
Love each other, for that is where Jah's spirit lives.
Love each other, Natty Dread.

Put down the gun, me say to put down the gun . . .

Rudy's captivating lyrics fill Tionne's, pulling everyone into the moment, myself included. When the chorus hits hard, we all join in singing, waving the green, gold and red Rastafari flag and chanting, 'Jah Rastafari.'

Even after I leave, the sounds of the crowd echo in my mind. I feel lighter, almost renewed, by the Rastafarian spirit, filled with a deep sense of peace and love in my heart. It hasn't just been a thought-provoking night – it feels like I've glimpsed something much deeper: a tight-knit community, grounded in history, culture and connection. For a moment, right here in England, I felt completely transported. I feel truly blessed to have been part of it – even if only for one night.

As I walk home, I keep thinking about my conversation with Rudy and Clive. Their views on life, identity and culture really stick with me. It's clear their experiences in Britain have been shaped by their strong Jamaican roots, but also by the racism they faced when they arrived in Britain. That mix of challenges has made them who they are: resilient and determined to build a better life.

I am especially inspired by the stories of entrepreneurship – like Mr T's daring venture with Tionne's. It's grown into way more than just a business; it's become a lively community hub and a proud symbol of culture and hope, standing strong even when violence threatens the neighbourhood.

But beneath those stories, I feel a real tension between the generations. Rudy and Clive spoke about the younger generation in Northville with some worry. They compared their own tough experiences to what they see today, believing that youth are drifting away from their culture, caught up in more Western ways of living. They warned that in chasing the trappings of modern life the young people might lose the strong spirit and work ethic that once held the community together.

Reflecting on the differences between generations, I've come to see that even though times have moved on, not much has really changed. The struggles Rudy, Clive and Mr T went through are still here – just in different forms. The mandem today are trying to find their way through a world that's messy and uncertain, and most of the time they're figuring it out with little guidance. Their path to adulthood feels unsteady – independence keeps getting pushed further out of reach, and the pressure to make it is constant. They're trying to carve out who they are in today's Britain, grappling with systemic barriers and the pull of the roads.

CHAPTER 8

Bookies

I'm heading to meet Anthony at the bookie's this humid summer afternoon. It's a familiar spot for him, as he makes the trek from his home in South London every week to place his bets. Anthony has always had a weakness for gambling, though he keeps it discreet. Ever since he had a big win with a horse named Cherish last year, he's convinced that luck is always on his side. The mandem and I see it differently, though. We view his gambling as more of an addiction, and a single stroke of luck doesn't change that.

Bookies are a common sight along the many high streets in London, and around Northville. The closest one to the estate is mainly frequented by older men in the community. On sweltering summer days like today, the place is alive with activity. It's far more than just a venue for placing bets. It is a bustling meeting point where men immerse themselves in passionate and heated debates, share stories and perhaps seek refuge from the weight of the world outside. Yet, beneath the lively conversations, lies a complex web of unfulfilled dreams, broken promises and personal sorrow. I've always viewed the bookie's as a kind of toxic haven, a gathering spot where many men find themselves if they don't abandon the roads. They don't die, they don't go to prison and they don't turn to religion. It's a sobering truth that the community has learned to accept as part of our reality.

'Finally decided to grace us with your presence, ay? Were you dolling yourself up just to come to the bookie's?' Anthony jokes as soon as he sees me. His jokes can be hit or miss, ranging from clever to cringeworthy.

'Are you serious? You're a real joker,' I reply, pointing to my casual skinny jeans and vest top.

Despite his impeccably put-together appearance, I find it amusing that he jokes about my clothes. He's dressed in luxurious designer brands from head to toe, complete with sleek black sunglasses more suited for a fashion show runway than a casual visit to the bookies. Among the modestly dressed men outside the bookmaker's, struggling to make ends meet, Anthony's clothing makes him stand out starkly. It's hard to overlook the parallel between his gambling addiction and his relentless pursuit of the most extravagant designer clothing.

Inside the bookie's, scuffed white walls enclose the space and blue iron tables are firmly bolted to the floor. Bright red plastic seats and litter bins add colour to the otherwise drab interior. But what strikes me first is the heavy smell in the air. The struggling air conditioning barely manages to cool the room, doing little to reduce the stale, suffocating atmosphere.

The group of elderly men are all engrossed in the multiple screens that hang on the walls, eagerly waiting to see how their bets turn out. Behind the large glass screen separating her from the customers, a tired-looking woman is advising a drunk man to leave, warning him she'll call the police if he doesn't. Just then, Anthony walks up, hands her his betting slip, and strikes up a conversation with her. His easy charm brings a smile to her face, and she playfully suggests he should call her later, hinting that this isn't the first time he's macked on her.

'You've got to be kidding me,' Anthony mutters as disbelief registers on his face. His smile quickly disappears and he carefully scrutinizes the older man who has just walked into the bookie's. 'What the hell are you doing in here? I thought you stopped coming here,' Anthony barks at his dad, Steve, as he turns to face him.

'Don't budda telling me what to do. What are you doing here? Why aren't you in the South?' Steve replies, shrugging off his coat as he hangs it behind his seat.

Anthony doesn't talk much about his relationship with his dad, but I get the impression that their connection is complex and strained when he does. Steve was not very present during Anthony's childhood, as he was often hustling to provide for his family. When he did spend time with Anthony, he was emotionally distant and preoccupied with his next sale.

Steve hustled for years, even during Anthony's teenage years when his son was old enough to notice what his dad did for a living. After getting expelled from school and spending more time with friends on the estate, Anthony followed in Steve's footsteps and started selling. Anthony has two children and expresses to everyone his desire to be a good father. He's told me he wants to give his children the attention he didn't have growing up. Sadly, trapping on the roads doesn't leave him much time to spend with his sons. He's aware of the risk of repeating the same patterns from his past, but can't seem to break free from them.

As I watch their heated argument, with Anthony angry about Steve's visit to the bookie's but also wrestling with unresolved feelings toward his dad, I can't help but notice the strong similarities between them and the intricate ways the intergenerational transmission of road life has rippled through the family, now manifesting in Anthony's life.

While Caribbean immigrants like Clive and Rudy managed to secure legitimate employment upon their arrival in England, the experiences of many other West Indian immigrants were starkly different. Numerous immigrants found themselves overqualified for the menial jobs – often characterized as 'slave labour' – offered by the British economy. Jamaican sociologist Ken Pryce observed this phenomenon in his influential work *Endless Pressure*.[1] Through rich ethnographic research in St Paul's, Bristol, Pryce explores the complex dynamics of race, racism and immigration that shaped the post-war experiences of first-generation West Indian immigrants, and their second-generation children. He addresses the harsh realities of life in the 1970s, highlighting the community's resilience and struggles. Pryce draws attention to several subcultures within the community, including 'Hustlers', who, compelled by 'endless pressure' and relentless structural constraints, resorted to finding alternative, often illegal opportunities outside the formal labour market to make ends meet and provide for their families.

During our conversation at Tionne's, Rudy spoke about the challenges facing men of his generation who didn't work in the legitimate economy, expressing that they had failed to set a positive example for their children. He said, 'Children will suffer the consequences of their parents' choices.' I am struck by his words as I watch the tense relationship between Steve and Anthony.

It is painfully apparent to me that Steve, lost in his own battles, can't guide Anthony towards a different path because he is trapped in the same struggles. He couldn't give his son the opportunities or the social or educational advantages he didn't have, and now Anthony carries the weight of that history, that identity and the hardships of being on road. Sadly, if he doesn't break free from this cycle, these burdens will likely be passed down to his children.

The tension between Anthony and Steve finally reaches its breaking point, and they take their argument outside. Anthony confronts his dad, yanking the crumbled betting slip from Steve's hand. With a mix of frustration and concern in his voice, he asks, point blank, if he has bothered to check on Ms Latimore, Anthony's sick mother. Despite their separation years ago, Steve had always tried to look after her, especially after Anthony had moved to South London. But Steve, now retired, spends most of his time at the bookie's, much to Anthony's dismay. As the confrontation escalates, Steve's friends intervene, trying to mediate the situation, but Anthony's frustration gets the better of him. He dismisses them sharply, commanding they stay out of his business. In a moment of exasperation, Steve turns and walks away, shuffling down Kurt Street in defeat.

'I love my dad. He just knows how to push my buttons. Do you think I was disrespectful? Sometimes, I get angry, thinking if I weren't raised in the slums, if he didn't hustle, maybe I would be different. But I didn't have to go down the same path.'

Anthony sounds exhausted as he talks. I realize that any advice or encouragement about changing his life will fall on deaf ears because he is deeply invested. He acknowledges this in his self-assessment, recognizing his agency and role in deciding to trap. He is opening up – or waking up – laying everything on the table. Engaged in my conversation with

Anthony, I suddenly spot a familiar face in the busy crowd outside the bookie's. He's parked outside the shop with his boombox, passionately repeating the same sad chorus:

> *Life in the concrete jungle is peak . . .*
> *Life in the concrete jungle, man can't sleep.*

'Look at him. I can't believe he's let himself go like this. Do you remember how respected he used to be back in the day? Now look at this madman,' Anthony comments with a hint of disdain, pointing towards Bailey, who is cussing out a group of men for not paying attention to the lyrics he's trying to share.

In the years following 1997, when he stood in the basketball cage with a loaded gun, defending himself from rivals, his life seemed to spiral from one tragedy to the next. A significant turning point came in the early 2000s when he was handed a lengthy prison sentence. Bailey wasn't quite the same after his release. He tried to resume his life as a drug dealer but failed. This marked the beginning of his battle with depression, which was compounded by the trauma of losing his friend, BK, to gun violence. His losses were dulled by weed and alcohol, leading him further into depression and to lingering outside the bookie's, where he would sing his favourite song every day to a laughing and mocking crowd.

Anthony looks at Bailey with disappointment as Bailey takes small sips from a concealed can of beer, the crumpled brown paper bag barely hiding it from view. Seeing someone drink beer from a brown paper bag in our neighbourhood has always been met with a sense of disgrace. It often reminds people of Max, the infamous drunkard, whose behaviour became a cautionary tale that no one wanted to follow as they grew up.

Bailey is wearing torn and dirty Nike joggers and a stained white jacket. His nose is caked with dried snot, and his body is sweaty. Gone are the days when he exuded an air of refinement, dressed in the latest designer clothes, flaunting Rolex watches, and with his hair and beard impeccably groomed.

'You really don't have to be so harsh, Anthony,' I remark, shaking my head in disappointment at how he describes Bailey. He no longer embodies the idealized image of being on road that Anthony once admired, and I can sense that this change is bothering him. Bailey has stopped living by the survival motto of 'getting money by any means', and in Anthony's eyes Bailey has fallen from grace. Tragically, he has no safety net to catch him.

As I approach Bailey, a silent turmoil takes root within me as I become more conscious of the silent battles with mental health brought about by the roads and how it gradually breaks people down.

Bailey looks me up and down, his eyes narrow, but with a smile on his face. Yet his guarded eyes tell a different story. He has stopped singing and instead starts rambling, with his words following a discernible pattern. He speaks of his baby mothers, then reminisces about his time making P with the mandem, repeatedly saying, 'They know. They know,' for the next few minutes. I say hello again, and this time I capture his gaze, and he recognizes me.

'Ebony, what's up, man? Where is Lorrie?'

Bailey's memory takes him back to our childhood, when Lorrie and I would play basketball with him in the cage. I try to keep him in that memory, but he starts to mutter again.

'Bailey, do you remember how great you were at basketball? Do you remember the medal you won when you beat the Eagles?'

As I remind Bailey of our younger days, time seems to stand still. He's hanging on to my every word, and I catch myself painting a detailed picture of the Bailey I used to know. I find myself talking to him about our intense battles playing 'round the clock' – a game that tested our shooting accuracy from different spots on the court. He always came out on top, playfully teasing us when we'd lose a game. The girls in the neighbourhood adored him, especially when he wore his yellow Lakers shorts and vest, accentuating his muscular arms as they peeked out. Even though he was five years older than us, he would watch us play rounders and runouts, joining in on the fun. Unlike the other older teenagers from our estate, he didn't take himself too seriously and embraced the moments of joy.

My eyes are now fixed on his, trying to conjure up an image of the younger basketball-loving teenager before the harsh realities of the roads altered his path, crushing his dreams of playing basketball professionally, as Lorrie had envisioned. Back in the day, Bailey had a heart of gold, which is why Lorrie cared for him so much. I vividly recall when he lent her his prized possession: a legendary BMX bike, equipped with a booming stereo, colourful flags and reflectors. He had spray-painted it, turning it into a unique piece of art. Lorrie kept it for a whole month, refusing to return it, but Bailey didn't mind; he had plenty of bikes on standby. Together, Bailey, Lorrie and Jacks raced through the estate, their laughter ringing out as they competed, just like they did in their basketball games.

I can still picture the day Lorrie pranked Bailey, pretending his favourite bike was stolen. The look of panic on his face is something I'll never forget as he searched every inch of the estate, desperately trying to find it. Lorrie was in stitches, dragging out the joke for days. Even after Bailey found out it was a prank, he couldn't help but laugh along with her. Of course, Bailey got his revenge a couple of weeks later. He hid Lorrie's beloved dog, Unity, for a few hours. Watching her frantically search for Unity was hilarious, especially since she's usually so composed. Thankfully, Bailey returned the dog just a few minutes later to calm her down. Their friendship was full of fun and playful teasing, and it was wonderful to witness.

Looking back, I can't help but admire the teenager he was – full of promise, humour and quiet kindness. I still think about the man he might've become. The memories of those days feel faint now, like echoes, but they haven't left me.

Something shifts in Bailey when I mention BK, and a flicker of recognition crosses his face as he utters: 'They know . . . They know . . . They know who did it.' His eyes pierce through me.

Reaching into his pocket, he pulls out a photo of the two of them together. Looking at me, he says, 'BK is my G. Do you remember when we used to DJ at Grove's Youth Club? We were young, but we were the baddest DJs in the hood. He's dead, you know. The last time I saw him, we were linking two gal.' For the first time, I catch a glimpse of the old Bailey, but he can't hold on to that moment and slips away again, starting to sing, *'Life in the concrete jungle is peak . . . Life in the concrete jungle, man can't sleep.'*

I stand beside him, listening as he repeats the same lines of the song over and over, nodding my head to the beat blasting from the boombox. Singing feels like a lifeline for him – a way to stay afloat in the middle of his battles with mental health and in the grip of alcoholism. Each note provides a brief moment of relief from the pain, helping him manage the heavy feelings of loss and the ugliness he's seen on the roads. I stay close because he needs someone to connect with, and I want him to know that I see him and I hear him, even though he feels like a shadow of who he used to be, in a world that barely acknowledges him and a community that seems to have forgotten his value.

Bailey's story is just one of many tragic tales that come out of the brutal and unforgiving world of the roads. Many men turn to substances like drugs or alcohol to numb the pain of their experiences. A common thread among them is the sense of alienation from their communities, especially when the reputations they once held are stripped away.

Take, for instance, Jacks's cousin Frankie, who was shot a couple of years ago. The incident shattered Frankie's sense of security and pushed him into deep anxiety and depression. Once celebrated for making serious money on road, Frankie now struggles financially. His days are mostly spent in front of his PlayStation, using video games to escape reality and shield himself from the harsh judgements outside.

Others, like Lukey – Cassius's cousin – also battle mental-health issues. As the money from drug dealing dried up, Lukey lost his financial independence, his reputation and his sense of purpose, leaving him feeling lost and unsure about the future. These men are the fallen soldiers of the roads – men who came of age in a world that glorified quick fixes and instant gratification, but who now face the hard truth: life without the roads, without the recognition that once defined them. For many, the way back feels impossible. Worse still, they remain trapped in a lifestyle that never prepared them for anything beyond it.

'Let's go, man. I need to head back to the endz to buck Cassius,' Anthony says with urgency as he joins Bailey and me.

'Bailey, you good?' he asks, refusing to make direct eye contact with him.

At first, Bailey doesn't seem to notice that Anthony is there. Then, out of nowhere, he stops singing and says: 'What's up, Julian?'

Julian is Anthony's older brother, who used to hang out with Bailey back in the day.

'It's Anthony, not Julian, but I'll let him know you said yo,' Anthony answers, feeling uneasy as he notices Bailey's fragile state.

Bailey briefly stares at Anthony before resuming his singing.

'This is exactly why I didn't wanna come over. I don't want to see him like this. Why didn't you just come when I first called you?' Anthony snaps, clearly upset by how distressed Bailey looks. 'Come on, let's go,' Anthony insists again, his frustration showing.

Turning to Bailey, I lean in and touch his shoulders. He briefly pauses his singing as he feels my touch. But when I bid him farewell he retreats into his world, a world that seems to shut us out and doesn't respond to my goodbye. As Bailey fades into the distance, Anthony and I walk back to Northville along Grimshaw Street. We see Mel, who is homeless, at her usual spot outside the local fish-and-chip shop. She approaches us and asks for a pound.

Without a second thought, Anthony pulls a five-pound note from his pocket and invites her to join him inside the shop. I'm surprised by this kind gesture, especially because he treats Mel so differently from Bailey. Both struggle with alcohol and mental-health challenges, so I can't help but wonder why he extends compassion towards one and not the other. The question weighs heavily on my mind, and I feel compelled to speak up.

'Why were you so unkind to Bailey? I could see you were uncomfortable with him. Why?' I ask.

His response is quick and defensive, as if I've hit a nerve. 'Just gimme me a sec. I'm gonna buy her a munch. I'm not giving her the money so she can go and smoke it away.' A few moments later, Anthony and Mel come out of the chip shop, with Mel holding a large paper bag full of chips, a sausage and a patty. While Mel enjoys her meal, Anthony and I pass around a bag of chips as we walk past the local food bank. There's a large crowd gathered outside, made up of people of all ages who desperately need food. The soft sobbing of an elderly woman touches Anthony, and he lets out a heavy sigh and looks at the long line of tired faces in front of us; I can feel his unease.

'I can't end up like that,' he declares with conviction. 'I won't be outside the bookie's, queuing at no food bank, or begging for a pound.'

I see this as a chance to connect the dots. 'Is that why you couldn't even give Bailey the grace he deserved?' I press gently, hoping to understand his harshness towards someone who clearly triggers him.

He rolls his eyes. 'I wasn't rude to him,' he insists, fidgeting with his lighter. 'I just . . .' He pauses to light his spliff, inhaling deeply as he collects his thoughts. 'Bailey had it all back in the day, the gal, the P, the cars. I heard he even bought a yard outside the endz. I'm just pissed with him. How could he let that all go? He's given up, man. He won't fight.'

'He can't fight,' I reply, knowing that both he and Bailey struggle with their problems, just in different ways.

'This is why man jeopardize their freedom and trap,' he responds. 'Well, that's why I do it. Nothing has been able to pull me away from the roads – not prison, not even the birth of my kids, not even the violence. I'm not scared to die, but I'm proper scared to end up like Bailey, with shit to show for myself.'

'You know the roads have an expiry date,' I remind him.

'Yeah, I know,' he replies, worry lines forming on his forehead as he contemplates it. 'I've been thinking about that a lot lately. I mean, what if I don't make it? What if I don't stack enough P to retire? So many mandem don't finish the race, and I'm starting to worry about that.'

As I study his face, I see a mix of uncertainty, fear and vulnerability. Despite his outward appearance of success, his inner life reflects a growing anxiety and a sense of looming doom. At thirty-three, he's realizing that his lifestyle is reaching its limits and that he needs to consider the potential consequences if he doesn't make a change.

'What would you do if you weren't trapping?' I enquire, curious about his unfulfilled dreams.

'Bloody hell,' he says, his eyes wide with surprise. 'I don't think anyone's ever asked me that before.' He smiles. 'You know, the saddest thing, I don't have a clue.'

'What did you want to be when you were a kid,' I press.

He laughs. 'That feels like such a long time ago. I used to

pretend I was a shopkeeper, so, yeah, maybe a shopkeeper or a businessman.'

'There is still time, Anthony,' I encourage him with a smile.

'Do you think I'll ever get out?' He turns to me with longing in his eyes.

'How ready are you to get out?' I question.

'I've been ready. I just don't know how to make that step,' he says quietly.

We continue to stroll down Grimshaw Street, taking in the scene around us. Nearby, men lean against walls or sit on steps, alert and tense, caught up in the daily grind – hustling, trapping, always watching for the next move. The air smells of cigarette smoke, fried food and cars passing by. The noise and movement never stop. This is the world we know – it's not calm, but it's normal, a rhythm we've always lived with.

'Look at where we've grown up, surrounded by trappers. I don't know how to be a normal civilian,' Anthony mutters, nodding towards the group of men across the road.

He lets out a heavy sigh, as if he has been holding this feeling inside for so long. 'It's easier to hit the roads – it's the easy option. If mainstream was easy, all the mandem would be doing it.'

His shoulders slump as he rubs the back of his neck. 'There's a lot of studying that has to go into changing. And look at me – I'm a big man now. Who's gonna put a roof over my head when I'm doing that?'

Frustration starts to creep into his voice. 'Listen, I wanna change. But I can't work for pennies in some shit job and that's the only option available right now if I was to get out.

I can't be a nobody.' And I can feel his every word – the fear of becoming invisible. On the roads, he's recognized. In the trap, he matters.

The silence after he admits his feelings hangs heavy between us, thick with tension. Then suddenly, out of nowhere, a burst of laughter pulls us from our conversation as Little Remi, a football tucked under his arm, and his friends race by. Little Remi bumps into Anthony on purpose, flashing a grin before darting ahead of us as we turn on to Greenery Avenue, the road that leads to Cassius's house, our next stop. Anthony's lips twitch into a half-smile, and his eyes soften as he calls out Little Remi's name. For a brief moment, he seems less burdened, like Little Remi's carefree energy pulls him back to a time before the trap's hold. But, just as quickly, that smile disappears, and his expression hardens again as he turns back to me.

'I can't rely on those dead-end jobs,' he says. 'They offer no guarantees. At least in the trap, I decide how much P I make.' He pauses, quiet for a moment, before continuing.

'When you're young, it's about garms, jewellery, clubbing, showing off. But when you get older your priorities change. You want a house and to be more independent. But you know you don't have the qualifications to make it in the mainstream, so you just stay on the roads and go hard.'

He shakes his head slowly. 'I know I can't do this forever. I don't want to. But I can't suffer either. Ask any of the mandem – no one wants to live like this. Looking over your shoulder. Getting caught up in madness. Going to prison. But right now the roads is all I have.'

His voice lowers, sounding haunted. 'Man trap, but don't

expect to be in it forever; man just gets sucked in. When you're in, it feels like there's no way back to society. No second chances for people like us.'

He briefly closes his eyes, as if trying to shut something out. 'And then you have all this stuff going through your mind – you've been through these wars on the roads – and you don't even know how to deal with it. How does man enter the mainstream with all that and then try to operate in that world?'

His tired eyes find mine again, open and vulnerable. 'We're trapped, man. Can't dream about the future you can't even see.'

'And what does that future look like?' I ask, even though I know how hard it is for him to picture one.

'Not being trapped in this shit – I'll tell you that much. Sometimes, I wish I'd never got involved. I just want to live a decent life – you know, that life with a house with a picket fence, somewhere out of London, with a bloody dog, two kids, a wife. On a deep one, I just wanna get away from the hood. I'll be forty before you know it. I need to think about my next moves, figure out how to get out and stay out.' He dreams openly, his expression softening.

As Anthony talks about leaving the roads behind, I catch a flicker in his eyes – a fragile glimmer, as if he's just beginning to imagine a different future. I find myself hoping he holds on to that small light and recognizes the burdens his dad, Steve, bore, as well as the daily struggles Bailey faces. The lingering presence of the dark mark that traverses generations hangs in the air as we pause outside Cassius's house before parting ways.

As Anthony walks away, I'm hit by the vulnerability in

men his age – men weighed down by past choices they can't take back. They're wrestling with existential questions about what life might hold beyond the roads, if they ever manage to take the leap into mainstream society. This transition isn't easy, especially for those without the support systems needed to build a new life. The visible consequences, like street violence, barely scratch the surface of the silent suffering beneath. The aftermath, the destinies of those on the roads, often go unnoticed by the world.

Yet, despite Anthony's struggles, my heart is filled with quiet optimism – that he is awakening, that he is becoming conscious. I carry that hope not only for him, but also for all the mandem yearning for a future abundant with possibilities and a life free from the constraints of the roads.

CHAPTER 9

Church

Ten years later, I'm at church on a bright spring day – the kind of day that makes you appreciate the beauty around you. For the first time this year, the sun is shining in Northville, sending warm light streaming through the tall windows of the church hall. Soft patches of sunlight scatter across the worn wooden floorboards, blending with the low hum of conversation.

We've all gathered to celebrate a joyful occasion: Bella's third child, Lia, is being welcomed into the community at her christening reception. Vicar William is here, quietly showing the new Vicar Francis the ropes – though he hardly needs the help, having confidently led the church for years since Vicar William stepped down. Vicar William feels as timeless as the church itself – steady, familiar and an essential part of the community. Even though he's enjoying quieter days with his wife, Irene, he still makes his way to major community events – walking stick in hand and always making sure he gets a plate of his favourite curry mutton.

Looking around the hall, my heart fills with joy at how beautifully everything's come together. There's this easy warmth in the room, the kind that comes with familiar faces, soft laughter, kids darting between legs and community elders catching up in the corners like they haven't seen each other in years. Everyone's here – family and friends – and it just feels right. A real celebration of new beginnings.

Guests walk in through a lovely arch made of white and gold balloons, and, above, banners bearing baby Lia's smiling face hang a little unevenly, but that just makes it feel more personal, like something made with love, not for show. Pastel-coloured lanterns sway gently from the high ceilings, stirred by a light breeze drifting through open windows. The tables are decorated with fresh flowers – red and white roses arranged in delicate crystal vases that catch the sunlight, making the room smell sweet. That fragrance blends perfectly with the warm, buttery smell of freshly baked cake, proudly displayed as the centrepiece on the large table near the stage.

Somewhere close by, a glass clinks softly, capturing everyone's attention. 'Let's raise a toast to my beautiful new niece!' Andy says, clearing his throat. His voice is steady, though there's a slight hint of nervousness. He stands at the polished wooden podium on stage, resting his fingers lightly on the edge, preparing to give what feels like the most important speech of his life. As the chatting quiets down and chairs gently scrape against the floor, the audience settles in. He exhales slowly and scans the crowd of familiar faces. There's a brief moment when the room seems to hold its breath, waiting for him to start. Then he begins to speak. His words are simple and meaningful, filled with memories, little stories and moments of family life that evoke soft laughter and a few teary eyes. There's something in the way he speaks – it's not rehearsed, just honest – making the moment feel both intimate and shared for everyone present.

After finishing his speech, a gentle wave of applause fills

the room, stretching the moment just a little longer. Andy steps down from the podium with a polite smile, shaking hands and accepting congratulations. But beneath the surface I sense something tugging at him – something feels off. I catch a fleeting look in his eyes as he glances away from the crowd, a hint of fatigue quickly masked by his practised smile.

As he makes his way towards my table, he bumps into a chair, and I hold back a smile, sensing he's not quite himself. When he finally reaches me, he pulls me into a warm hug, and I catch the sharp scent of rum on his breath – clearly, he's had a few too many drinks.

'Your speech was on point,' I tell him, looking into his eyes. He nods and grins back at me.

'Well, I do try,' he responds, pretending to take a bow. But his laughter sounds forced, and the easy confidence he had onstage starts to wane.

I ask where Cassius is, thinking he might be the next one to take the spotlight as Lia's godfather. Suddenly, Andy's face tightens, and his earlier light-heartedness disappears. He looks me dead in the eye and drops the bombshell: 'Didn't you hear? Cassius is in prison.'

His words hit me hard, almost making me choke on my mocktail, which suddenly feels thick and hard to swallow. I struggle to take in what he is saying. Just a month ago, I saw Cassius at Vinnies's, and he was excited about his new steady job in construction.

I can still vividly remember how animated he was when he talked about working hard, saving up money and eventually buying a house, where he could feel safe. That conversation felt monumental, as if he was on the brink of a big change. But this, hearing about his latest drug charge, feels like a blow – like all the hope I had for him has been crushed in a moment.

The happy vibe around me feels suddenly out of place after this hard-hitting news. I sit with it, thinking hard, realizing that the roads still hold Cassius captive, just as they've trapped so many others. Even with the glimpse of optimism I saw in him that day, it has always been painfully clear how hard it is for Cassius – the mandem – to picture a life beyond Northville. After all, it's in Northville where they discover the roads, or where the roads find them. It's where identities take shape, where their view of the world gets fixed early. And, once that happens, it's hard to picture life any other way.

I've always thought of the roads as a cruel paradox – offering shelter to the mandem, acting as a lifeline in many ways, yet at the same time trapping them in a cycle of dependency that feels impossible to break. The lifestyle clings to them like a heavy burden, leaving scars that run deep, changing their lives and dimming their futures. True freedom feels like a distant dream, always just out of reach for those caught in the struggles of the roads.

As I sit across from Andy, I watch him down shot after shot of tequila, the clear liquid disappearing fast, and I can see his hands start to shake. With each gulp, he seems to sink deeper into a heavy mood. An uncomfortable silence lingers between us until he finally speaks.

'I can't catch a break,' he says, his voice tight. 'No matter what I do, I just can't change.'

I open my mouth to say something to comfort him, but he waves me off, as if my words mean nothing right now. 'Talking doesn't help,' he insists. He hesitates, jaw tightening, then continues. 'Bella and Mum are always on my case, telling me I need to sort out my life, but they don't understand. I can't keep up with the expectations any more. I can't come through for them,' he admits, downing another shot.

I'm reminded, with a quiet heaviness, of what Bella said about his struggles – how his family is starting to lose hope in him. After getting out of prison, he had promised to find work, but over the years he's broken those promises. Now, he isn't working at all – he's back on the roads. This has left his family disappointed and made it hard for them to trust that he can truly change. Family means everything to Andy. And I can only imagine that kind of disappointment – from the people who matter most – must be a heavy thing to carry. It's no surprise he looks so overwhelmed, facing challenges both seen and unseen.

Watching Andy like this is really tough; he looks completely lost and defeated. He stumbles towards the open bar, trying hard to stay on his feet. Meanwhile, the celebration goes on around us – music is loud, people are laughing and glasses are clinking. The twinkling fairy lights lighting up the dim hall create a warm, inviting atmosphere, casting a gentle glow on groups of friends chatting and smiling, fully caught up in the moment. But Andy isn't present, not really.

Just as I'm about to go over to Bella to ask her to keep an eye on him, Jacks walks in under the balloon arch. He looks amazed as he takes in the decorations – typical Jacks, always noticing the little things others miss. His excitement brightens the room, which is the complete opposite of Andy's heavy demeanour.

Jacks heads straight to the dancefloor as the DJ drops Iba Mahr's 'Great is H.I.M'. The steady base vibrates through the wooden floorboards, steady, grounding. From my seat, I watch him dance, moving easily and freely as he lets the music lead him. Around him, people sway — some with their eyes shut, others smiling like they've heard the song a thousand times before and still love it. There's something special about it — both heavy and peaceful at the same time, like a quiet prayer you can feel even if you can't hear it clearly. For a moment, I almost forget about Andy and am tempted to get up and let the music take me too.

Just as I'm about to step on to the dancefloor, the atmosphere in the room suddenly shifts — like the room loses its glow all at once. Aron and Ash burst into the hall like a whirlwind, drawing everyone's attention with their intense presence. Laughter and lively conversations die down almost instantly, replaced by a thick, uneasy silence as the music comes to a sudden stop.

Aron stands in the hall, looking nervous and tense. He scans the hall with worried eyes, searching for someone or something. Then he raises his voice, raw and urgent: 'I was just trying to get to my family! I can't believe this bullshit, these youts are taking the piss!' A fresh cut under his eye catches the light. Already, dark bruises are forming around it.

Leaning in close, he whispers something to Jacks, but the loud crowd drowns out his words. I see Jacks's face change as he reacts to what Aron just said. His fingers start to scratch at the eczema that has bothered him since we were kids — something that I always recognize as a sign that he's feeling anxious. The tension in the room grows heavier, almost suffocating. Without saying anything, Aron, Ash and a visibly shaky Andy slip away quickly, leaving everyone else standing there, confused and uneasy.

Jacks and I share a long look; there's a deep understanding

in his eyes that fills the space between us, even before he begins to explain.

'They attacked him,' he says quietly. 'It's a madness. He ain't even active any more in these postcode wars, but these youngers think they can get some clout by violating him, because his name still carries weight on road.'

'I'm heading out. You coming?' Jacks asks, nodding towards the exit where Bella is glued to her phone, frantically trying to locate both Aron and Andy.

I follow Jacks outside, pausing to gently touch Bella's shoulder and wave goodbye to Shelly and the rest of the family. They stand together, looking confused and worried, trying to wrap their heads around the chaos that just unfolded.

Once outside, the cool breeze brushes against my face, a welcome relief. Jacks turns to me, clearly upset. 'This is why I hate coming back to the endz,' he says. 'It just gives man PTSD. I wish I could stay in Barbados forever.'

I can relate to what he's feeling, so I nod in agreement. 'Yeah, I heard you've been travelling a lot. I love that for you.' Knowing he struggles with depression, I try to steer the conversation toward something more uplifting.

A hint of a small smile appears as his mood shifts a little. 'Mohammed got married a couple of months ago in Barbados,' he shares, sounding more cheerful. 'He's thinking about moving there permanently with his wife to be closer to family. I've been going back and forth with Nia, trying to spend time with my own family. On a level, I might just dig up myself. There's nothing left for me in Northville, and every time I come back I just feel lost.'

As we walk towards the block, Jacks picks up his pace, and I struggle to keep up with him. He starts to open up about what he's been feeling. 'It's been rough, the last few months,' he admits quietly. 'I've been applying for jobs everywhere, but haven't had any luck. I'm just starting to think what's the point of even trying any more.'

He stops for a moment to unbutton his crisp white shirt, revealing his frustration. 'I'm trying to stay on the straight and narrow, but when I'm not working, I have to trap to keep on top of things. Nia is getting more expensive every day.'

As we stop at the traffic lights, I spot Anthony sitting in his new high-spec BMW. 'Jump in,' he calls out, turning on to a side road. It suddenly hits me how long it's been since we last saw each other. The engine hums softly as we slide into the back seat.

'Cassius called me to tell me Aron was attacked,' he says, voice low and tense. I think about how fast news travels in the endz – how Cassius even found out so quickly, despite being locked up.

'It's madness,' Anthony continues, adjusting his tie – a rare sight, since I've never seen him wear a suit. 'Man's grown now, trying to do different things, but the roads don't sleep. They keep pulling man back.'

As we drive toward the block, Anthony tells us about his new job, which lets him to drive around the city in cars he once admired on posters on his bedroom wall. The leather seats, the impressive sound system and the smooth ride all shout success. But there's no excitement or sense of achievement in his voice – just a quiet sort of emptiness, as if he's achieved all his material dreams, but still feels lost inside.

'I feel like I have to wear the mask of a civilian,' he says quietly as we turn on to the block.

'It's not easy being in the real world when man is still in

the struggle. I'm still in the hood, still have the same friends; the same temptations are there, the violence, the bullshit. I'm around different people now, but sometimes I feel uncomfortable. Don't get me wrong, I hold my own, but they don't have a clue who I am outside work.'

Caught in a struggle between his past and his future, Anthony's challenges feel real and relatable. He is unsure about how to understand the changes happening within him or who he is turning into. It is a delicate situation: he wants to pursue new opportunities and dreams, but his old habits and insecurities keep pulling him back to where he started.

Around his new co-workers, he often feels out of place, as if he's still trying to figure out a language everyone else already knows. That makes him feel like a fraud next to people who seemed to have life all figured out, holding some secret to happiness he just hasn't found yet. Deep down, he wants more than just to fit in – he wants to be understood, without having to hide where he came from or act like his past didn't matter. Even though he wants to move forward, part of him holds on tight to what is familiar, not sure how to let go completely.

After a quick stop at Vinnie's, where Jacks grabs a bottle of Guinness, we finally pull up at the block. It's more packed than usual today, with cars lined up along the street and the mandem gathered in small clusters, showing their support for Aron. In the crowd, I spot Mrs Paula – ever the neighbourhood matriarch – talking quietly with Aron. Her presence seems to ease his anxiety. I notice the gentle way her eyes crinkle with concern, and I see him starting to relax as they share what looks like a deep and healing conversation. It's a comforting reminder of how much she means to all of us – a guiding force that keeps the community strong, even when things around us feel like they're falling apart.

As we approach, Ash sees us and calls out, 'What's good, my peeps?' Then he turns to Jacks and asks, 'You got that ting lined up yet?' It's clear he's referring to some sort of drug deal. I've watched Ash navigate the drug economy with caution, always managing to keep a safe distance. He'd be doing all right for a while, working at a local supermarket, talking about saving for his place. But lately I've noticed the change: fewer smiles, more silence, more time around certain people. Today, he seems distracted and uneasy.

'Is everything okay? Are you lot alright?' I ask.

Ash looks at me, but his face shows nothing. His eyes are dull, and his jaw is tense. 'You know how it is. Same old shit.' He shrugs, trying to act nonchalant, but it doesn't work. His voice is monotone and it feels as if he's recited those words too many times before.

'Run me my man's number. I'll shout him myself,' Ash says, his tone sharper this time. When Jacks gives him the number, he quickly pulls out his phone, typing with an urgency that feels familiar. There's a restlessness in the way he shifts his weight, like something inside him won't settle. He doesn't have to say it. I already know. You always know. It's in the eyes, the energy, in the quiet desperation people carry when they're trapped again – when the roads have them again.

Jacks and I make our way through the crowd, passing small groups of mandem deep in conversation. We head straight for Aron, who's just finished talking to Mrs Paula.

Jacks spuds him, and I ask how he's holding up. Aron seems more at ease than he did earlier at the church hall – Mrs Paula must've really worked her magic on him.

'I'm okay, just shocked to be honest,' he replies with a light laugh, though his eyes are still alert, scanning the area, as if he hasn't fully realized that he is safe now. 'These youngers had me running for my life. Haven't moved like that in years.'

He shakes his head, half amused, half in disbelief. 'I won't let them draw me out, though. I came close to riding out, but I've got too much to lose now.' He points to his son, Amir, who is happily riding his bike through the crowd.

Aron became a father five years ago, which came as a surprise to many of us. He'd always said he wasn't cut out for it, especially given how deep he was in the roads. But when Amir was born something changed in him. You could see it in the way he moved. It was slower, more intentional – as if he finally had something important worth holding on to.

'It's just bullshit,' he says, his voice dropping. 'But you know the wickedest ting? I was that younger once – trying to get stripes, make a name. It's a vicious cycle, and if you're lucky you make it to the other side. I did.'

There's a sense of relief in his voice, but it's also heavy with responsibility. 'My priorities have changed. I've got to keep working, show my son a different life. I don't want him growing up seeing the things I've seen. But it's fucked. I'll always be a target because of who I violated in the past and who man is.'

Listening to him, his words land hard. It's striking how some things never really change – how violence still follows Aron, no matter how far he thinks he's come. The roads don't forget, and old reputations cling on, drawing trouble even when someone's trying to start fresh. As I watch him calling after his son, who is oblivious to his struggles, I sense a mix of pride and worry in his eyes – it's like he's holding two truths at once. No matter how much time goes by, or how far someone believes they've moved on, the past can always catch up, catching you off guard and reminding you that some battles never truly end.

I stay on the block for a while, watching the mandem move through the same familiar routines. Time has passed, but not much has changed – you can still see the struggles etched on their faces, silent stories they barely share out loud. Their challenges run deep, affecting everything: how they live, what they choose, what they think they can hope for. I find myself wondering how I'll ever put it all into words – the pain, the cycles that seem impossible to break and the small, faint bit of hope that somehow still lingers underneath it all.

Right now, I'm deep in the middle of writing the book proposal, driven by a strong desire to share our stories – to make sure they're heard beyond the hood. But, standing here, I feel the heavy burden of responsibility pressing on my chest. I want to speak for the mandem, to shine light on what they've been through – and what they're still going through. But honestly I'm scared. How do I tell these stories in a way that feels real, with the care and sensitivity they deserve, without getting it wrong or missing the heart of what matters?

I turn to Jacks, feeling the need to share what's been on my mind. 'I just want to get it right. I want to tell your stories authentically, but it feels overwhelming,' I confess.

Jacks looks at me with intense, steady eyes, like he understands more than I've said out loud. 'Nobody can tell the story like you. You grew up in the slums too,' he says, his voice calm but firm. There's a certainty in his words and, somehow, it loosens the tightness in my chest.

'Just tell it like it is, Ebs,' he encourages. His words ground me, reminding me how important this journey really is. As I leave the block that day, surrounded by lively conversations, still worried about the futures of those I care for, yet I hold on to Jacks's mantra – 'Just tell it like it is' – knowing it will help me navigate the challenging path ahead.

Epilogue

It's 2025, and I'm sitting at my messy desk, surrounded by a rainbow of sticky notes – each one scribbled with a different idea as I try to figure out how to wrap up this book. Despite my best efforts, I'm facing writer's block. I've taken Jacks's advice to 'tell it like it is' throughout the chapters, but now that I'm nearing the end I feel the pressure to give the mandem's stories a fitting conclusion. Their lives – so real and raw – don't come with neat, tidy endings.

In the quiet of my room, I remember a quote from Stephen King: 'The most important things are the hardest things to say.'[1] It hits me as I stare at the blank page, feeling the pressure build. This empty page seems to resist my efforts, daring me to dig deeper. Wanting to write the perfect ending only adds to the challenge, making it even harder to sum up this journey.

I reflect on all the insights and lessons I've learned from the mandem throughout our time together – the hilarious moments that made us laugh, the heart-wrenching challenges that deepened my understanding of the roads and the resilience they've shown in the face of adversities that would make many crumble. Each memory holds weight, shaping not just their stories but my own as well.

I think about myself in all this – Ebony, not just the insider, not just the academic researcher, but a human who has been part of this process and conscious of how the writing has impacted me. Ultimately, I realize that concluding this book isn't just about recapping their experiences, though that's part of it. It's about reaching something deeper – the raw emotions that have shaped my own journey, intertwined with the powerful stories I've been privileged to share.

Taking a deep breath, I let my thoughts flow on to the page, weaving my truth with that of the mandem, hoping these final words do justice to our shared experiences and how our lives in Northville have shaped who we are – sometimes in ways we don't fully see but always carry with us.

Telling this story has been a deeply emotional journey – one filled with stops and starts, long pauses, tears, confusion and even some lighter moments. I think I felt the full spectrum of human emotion and have sometimes questioned whether I could keep writing. Revisiting moments from my past that still reverberate in my life today stirred up more than I expected – and that's probably been the hardest part of it all. As I sit with that, I vividly picture my thirteen-year-old self, forever marked by the traumatic day when Bailey ran on to the basketball court. In an instant, everything changed. Street violence slammed into my world, shattering the unbreakable sense of safety that once wrapped around my childhood like a warm blanket. It was the first time I had ever seen a gun and heard the terrifying sound of gunshots. The memories of that fateful day are seared into my mind, serving as a painful reminder of the brutal truths we confronted growing up in Northville, where street violence, disturbingly, became an all-too-common aspect of our lives.

Despite holding on to some difficult memories, I can still

picture my younger self and those bright, sunny summers packed with laughter and adventure. My childhood friends back then – Lorrie, Neva, Cory and the ever-energetic Jacks – used to say those days were 'on fire', and for good reason. We spent endless hours soaking up the sunshine and the freedom of being young. I treasure those playful afternoons when we raced our bikes through the neighbourhood, had water fights that left us drenched and giggling, played games like rounders and run-outs and hung out in the basketball cage. That place became special for us, where our friendships grew strong and where we shared our dreams under the wide open sky, imagining all the possibilities that lay ahead. Our street parties, still celebrated today, were more than just gatherings; they were lively events filled with the delicious aroma of grilled food and good music, creating a wonderful sense of community among us.

As I reflect on my life in Northville – the past and the present, the good and the bad – I'm starting to understand just how deeply this place has shaped who I am. Some emotions don't disappear; they sit quietly in the background, waiting for the right moment to rise and be felt. Writing this story has helped me untangle some of those buried feelings – it's been a release. It's pushed me to face the questions that have been lingering in the corners of my mind, waiting to be acknowledged. It's also helped me make sense of things I didn't even realize I needed to say. Through this process, I've connected more deeply with my own truths, as well as the shared experiences that shape so many of us who grew up in the hood – and the marks they leave on our hearts and minds.

I've taken a different path in life compared to the mandem, yet we remain connected by the shared experience of growing up in a neighbourhood that exposed us to some of the darker and more unsettling sides of humanity. Each of us carries our own emotional weight, navigating an environment where moments of light are often overshadowed by long stretches of struggle.

But while our experiences overlap, the pressures and dangers the mandem faced as young boys and men on the estate weren't ones I had to confront. I was spared the need to prove myself in the same ways – to navigate the risks tied to masculinity, postcode wars and road reputation. My challenges were different – often quieter, sometimes unseen – but no less real. What I do know is that growing up in the hood shaped all of us. It shaped how we see the world, how we face adversity and how we chase opportunity.

In my case, the generational trauma woven into our environment sparked a relentless determination to free myself from the limits placed on us. I've committed to breaking the mental chains – the repetitive patterns and cycles that can feel impossible to escape. Living in Northville, where expectations are often low, became both a backdrop and a driving force behind my ambition. I dared to imagine a better future, one that felt possible because of the love, support and grounding influence of my family. That foundation, along with a strong work ethic and a belief in the value of education, has been central to my pursuit of upward mobility.

I don't share this to present myself as some kind of success story – someone who made all the right choices while the mandem didn't. The truth is, being human comes with its struggles, and that weight hits differently depending on your circumstances. I know I carry less trauma than many of the mandem, and that's given me the space to navigate life with a bit more lightness and freedom. That relative privilege has helped me chase my dreams and carve out a life that feels meaningful. You could say I've been engaged in that age-old alchemical quest of turning straw into gold — a pursuit grounded in hope and imagination. I have to be honest; I'm still in the process of weaving that straw. I haven't fully worked it out yet. I'm still navigating adulthood, carrying my own complexities, trying to find my footing in spaces that don't always reflect where I've come from. Each step brings its own challenges, reminding me that, while our experiences may differ, most of us are just trying to do the same thing, find where we belong. But I also recognize that the journey is even harder for the mandem. Imagine trying to make sense of your place in the world without the qualifications that open doors. Now imagine doing that in what sometimes feels like a war zone, where threats are constant, and rival groups are ready to pick up weapons, hunt you down and harm you. In the hood, the drug trade isn't some distant concept — it's right there on your doorstep, offering quick money and a glimpse of something better. But that path is lined with danger, and the consequences are often devastating. For many, that makes the dream of transformation not just difficult, but nearly impossible.

At the heart of being human is a simple need: to matter. To have our existence acknowledged and valued. That need cuts across all backgrounds, including those who find themselves on road. In a world where worth is too often measured by wealth, power and visibility, yet access to these is heavily gatekept, the roads can seem like one of the few ways to gain recognition. For many of the mandem, becoming a 'badman' or getting involved in trapping isn't solely about earning respect or making money, though these are important factors.

At a deeper level, it's about carving out a credible identity, and gaining some level of control over their destinies in a world where opportunities are few and far between.

In places like Northville, the need for respect goes beyond being just a value; it turns into a kind of power that carries a lot of sway. The allure of the roads is incredibly attractive because it offers immediate rewards, despite the associated risks. This path promises an elevated position that is difficult to resist. In their unending search for meaning and validation, boys and men from similar backgrounds often find themselves locked in fierce competition. This struggle becomes one of survival, not just for space or social standing, but for visibility, and, ultimately, the elusive feeling of self-worth for which everyone longs.

In writing this book, my intention was never to justify or excuse the violence and criminality that often accompany the lives of the mandem. Now that we've reached the end, my hope is that I've shown you the depths of their struggles — struggles far more complex than the simplified versions often portrayed in the news or by politicians and some experts. The mandem's reality is shaped by a tangled mix of present struggles and past traumas, trapping them in cycles that disconnect them from the futures for which they might dare to imagine and strive.

I do not claim to have all the answers to the complex issues surrounding street violence. This topic is vast and multifaceted, and this book only scratches the surface. In striving to shed light on this reality, I recognize that the lived experiences of those on road are rich and intricate, deserving far deeper understanding than words alone can convey. Through this book, I hope to have reframed the narratives of the mandem, infusing their stories with greater depth, and situating them within the broader context of their identities and the psychosocial forces that have shaped their paths. This is my contribution, and I sincerely hope these stories will not only enrich the conversation around street violence but also inspire greater insight and compassion in those who read them.

Acknowledgements

Big up, Northville! This place has been a foundational part of my life; without it, I wouldn't have lived the experiences that inspired me to write from the heart. I am beyond grateful to the mandem and community, who generously shared their stories and truths with me. This book exists because of your voices, and I hope I have represented your lives in a way that feels true to you.

I owe a special thank you to Marcel Theroux for kickstarting this journey. It's still surreal how the universe brought you to my research. I'll always treasure that twist of fate, your encouragement, and the pivotal role you played in opening the door for this story to reach the world. I'm also deeply thankful to Hannah Griffith for connecting me with literary agents – your support and contribution to this journey have not gone unnoticed.

Sophie Lambert, having you as my agent is yet another blessing. I truly hit the jackpot when we teamed up. From our very first conversation, you threw your passion behind me and this project, guiding me through uncharted waters with your exceptional expertise. Thank you for your unwavering support – I wouldn't have come this far without it. And to Alice Hoskyns, I appreciate the feedback on the drafts – your thoughtful suggestions really made the proposal shine.

Lemara Lindsay-Prince, I can't forget to give you your flowers. You championed the project from day one, understanding the essence of the stories and giving my vision a platform to grow. Your early creative insights helped shape the book, and I've deeply valued the authenticity of our collaboration – thank you!

ACKNOWLEDGEMENTS

Joelle Owusu, a massive thank you for expertly guiding me through those crucial final stages. Your dedication and willingness to listen ensured every detail aligned perfectly with my vision. I am immensely appreciative of you and the entire #Merky Books team who worked behind the scenes to facilitate the project's completion and bring it to life. Samantha Stewart, your efforts during the editing phase made all the difference – thank you for being such an awesome team player.

My inner circle, you know who you are. Thank you for all those emergency calls, inspiring conversations, and much-needed lunch dates that kept me laser-focused on the finish line. You've been my biggest cheerleaders, and I feel incredibly fortunate to have such an amazing tribe of like-minded friends in my corner.

Lastly, but definitely not least, I'm sending all my love and gratitude to my mum and siblings. Even as we carry the pain of losing Daddy – Mum, your other half – you have always found ways to celebrate me and every milestone along this journey. Thank you for being present and lifting me up when I needed it most. This achievement is not just mine – it belongs to all of us. Love ya!

Notes

INTRODUCTION

1. In her 2012 book, *Fitting into Place? Class and Gender Geographies and Temporalities*, Yvette Taylor uses the term 'place sameness' to describe how some locations are seen and experienced as unchanging, homogeneous, and fixed in character, often shaped by dominant cultural narratives and social frameworks related to class, gender, and identity.
2. See: White, J. (2020), *Terraformed: Young Black Lives in the Inner City*. London: Repeater Books, which offers an in-depth analysis of gentrification and its impact on urban communities, particularly through the lens of young Black lives in the inner city.
3. Trust for London (2024), *Borough-level poverty 2024*. Available at: https://trustforlondon.org.uk/data/poverty-borough/
4. Hallsworth, S., & Young, T. (2008), 'Gang talk and gang talkers: A critique.' *Crime, Media, Culture*, 4(2), 175–195. https://doi.org/10.1177/1741659008092327 (Original work published 2008).
5. Bar, C. (2017), 'Child knife deaths in England and Wales set for nine-year peak', *The Guardian*, 28 November. Available at: https://www.theguardian.com/membership/2017/nov/28/child-knife-deaths-in-england-and-wales-set-for-nine-year-peak
6. Warren, J. (2024), 'London: More teenagers killed in 2023 than 2022'. BBC News, 3 January. Available at: https://www.bbc.co.uk/news/uk-england-london-67863910
7. Office for National Statistics (2024), *Crime in England and Wales: year ending March 2024*. Available at: https://www.ons.

NOTES

gov.uk/peoplepopulationandcommunity/crimeandjustice/ bulletins/crimeinenglandandwales/yearendingmarch2024

8. The Ben Kinsella Trust, 'Knife Crime Statistics'. Available at: https://benkinsella.org.uk/knife-crime-statistics
9. Youth Endowment Fund (2025), *Racial disproportionality in violence affecting children and young people*. Available at: https://youthendowmentfund.org.uk/reports/racial-disproportionality/
10. David Gadd and Tony Jefferson are British criminologists who have made significant contributions to the field of psychosocial criminology. Their book *Psychosocial Criminology* (2007), highlights their research and findings.
11. BBC News (2022), 'Walworth park attack: Man "stabbed by knife-wielding gang"', 22 August. Available at: https://www.bbc.co.uk/news/uk-england-london-53874975
12. *Telegraph* (2024), 'Moment knife-wielding gang attack unfolds in back of taxi', 26 July. Available at: https://www.telegraph.co.uk/news/2024/07/26/watch-knife-wielding-gang-attack-man-back-taxi-london
13. BBC News (2022), 'County Lines: More than 4,000 Londoners identified in drugs gangs', 19 September. Available at: https://www.bbc.co.uk/news/uk-england-london-49751780
14. Check out Stanley Cohen's important work from 1972, *Folk Devils and Moral Panics*. In it, he examines how the media portrayed youth cultures in Britain during the 1960s.
15. The following link provides more details about the Gang Violence Matrix: https://www.met.police.uk/police-forces/metropolitan-police/areas/about-us/about-the-met/gangs-violence-matrix/

COTCH

1. *Dancehall Queen* is a Jamaican film released in 1997. It was directed by Don Letts and Rick Elgood.
2. Check out this link: https://www.medicalnewstoday.com/articles/age-regression to learn more about the idea of 'age regression'.

NOTES

3. Bignall, T., Jeraj, S., Helsby, E., and Butt, J. (2019), *Racial disparities in mental health: Literature and evidence review*. London: Race Equality Foundation. Available at: https://raceequalityfoundation.org.uk/wp-content/uploads/2022/10/mental-health-report-v5-2.pdf
4. Reset MH is a UK based charity that offers free mental health support to people in the Black community. This includes support groups specifically for men. You can find more information through their link. https://resetmh.co.uk/our-work/
5. Bakhtin, a renowned Russian philosopher, first introduced this idea in his famous works *Rabelais and His World* (1984b) and *Problems of Dostoevsky's Poetics* (1984a).

BLOCK

1. In his book *Code of the Street: Decency, Violence, and the Moral Life of the Inner City* (1999), Elijah Anderson uses the term 'decent families' to refer to those families who strive to uphold their values and morals, while working hard to improve their lives, even when confronted with difficult circumstances in their neighbourhoods.
2. The term gained recognition in criminology through Lea and Young's (1984) book, *What Is to Be Done About Law and Order?*. They explained it further in their 1985 book, *Relative Deprivation and Crime*.
3. Sandberg, S. (2008), 'Street capital: Ethnicity and violence on the streets of Oslo'. *Theoretical Criminology*, 12(2), 153–171. https://doi.org/10.1177/1362480608089238 (Original work published 2008).
4. Sullivan, B. (2024), 'Social Media Creates Unhappiness by Promoting Materialism', *Psychology Today*, 5 February. Available at: https://www.psychologytoday.com/gb/blog/pleased-to-meet-me/202402/social-media-creates-unhappiness-by-promoting-materialism

NOTES

SHUBS

1. Stolzoff, N.C. (2000), *Wake the Town and Tell the People: Dancehall Culture in Jamaica*. Durham, NC: Duke University Press.
2. Ilan, J., (2015), *Understanding Street Culture: Poverty, Crime, Youth and 'Cool'*. Basingstoke: Palgrave Macmillan.

TRAP HOUSE

1. White, N. (2024), 'Pupil exclusions soar as Black Caribbean and Traveller students kicked out of school at higher rates', 5 September. Available at: https://www.independent.co.uk/news/education/education-news/school-exclusions-black-caribbean-traveller-students-b2606996.html
2. For more details about the trapper typology, see my article: 'Trap Life: The psychosocial underpinnings of street crime in inner-city London', *The British Journal of Criminology*, Volume 63, Issue 1, January 2023, Pages 168–183. https://academic.oup.com/bjc/article/63/1/168/6544789
3. Klein, M. (1995), *The American Street Gang: It's Nature, Prevalence and Control*. New York: Oxford University Press.
4. Freud, S. (1920), *Beyond the Pleasure Principle*. Dover Publications INC.
5. *The Wire* is a highly praised American crime drama show created by David Simon, who used to work as a police reporter. It was broadcast on HBO for five seasons, running from 2002 to 2008.
6. Gilligan, J. (2003), 'Shame, Guilt, and Violence', *Social Research*, 70(4), pp. 1149–1180.
7. Winnicott, D. W. (1965), 'Ego Distortion in Terms of True and False Self'. In: *The Maturational Processes and the Facilitating Environment*. London: Hogarth Press.

NOTES

MOSQUE

1. I co-wrote an academic paper with Jonathan Ilan titled 'Deen and Dunya: Islam, Street Spirituality, Crime, and Redemption in English Road Culture'. You can find it here: https://journals.sagepub.com/doi/abs/10.1177/13624806231184172
2. Ministry of Justice (2021), 'Exploring the nature of extremism in 3 prisons: findings from qualitative research'. [online] London: Ministry of Justice. Available at: https://www.gov.uk/government/publications/exploring-the-nature-of-extremism-in-3-prisons-findings-from-qualitative-research

PEN

1. The dynamics of this moral panic were thoroughly examined by sociologists Stuart Hall and his colleagues in their influential work *Policing the Crisis: Mugging, the State and Law and Order* (1978), in which they highlight the intricate relationship between societal perceptions of crime and the implications for racial discourse during that time.
2. The Brixton Uprising, often referred to as the Brixton Riots, took place in April 1981 and was a significant event in recent British history.
3. The sus ('suspected person') law was based on an old law called the Vagrancy Act from 1824. One part of this law, known as Section 4, gave police the authority to stop and arrest anyone they thought was loitering with the intention of committing a crime.
4. Scarman, L. (1981), *The Scarman Report: The Brixton Disorders 10–12 April 1981*. London: HMSO.
5. Macpherson, W. (1999), 'The Stephen Lawrence Inquiry: Report of an Inquiry by Sir William Macpherson of Cluny'. London: The Stationery Office. Available at: https://www.gov.uk/government/publications/the-stephen-lawrence-inquiry
6. Lammy, D. (2017), 'The Lammy Review: An independent review into the treatment of, and outcomes for, Black, Asian and Minority Ethnic individuals in the Criminal Justice System'.

London: HM Government. Available at: https://www.gov.uk/government/publications/lammy-review-final-report
7. Casey, L. (2023), 'Baroness Casey Review: An independent review into the standards of behaviour and internal culture of the Metropolitan Police Service'. London: Home Office. Available at: https://www.met.police.uk/police-forces/metropolitan-police/areas/about-us/about-the-met/bcr/baroness-casey-review/
8. Public Health England (2021), *Public Health Outcomes Framework: Reoffending rates*.

SHEBEEN

1. The 2008 financial crisis, commonly known as the Global Financial Crisis (GFC), was the most severe economic downturn since the Great Depression of the 1930s, resulting in a worldwide recession. Its effects continue to be felt today across economies, politics and societies worldwide.
2. This quote comes from Dr Gabor Maté's book *In the Realm of Hungry Ghosts*, which was published in 2008. In this book, he explores the subject of addiction and emphasizes the importance of understanding how past traumatic experiences can influence people's struggles with addiction.
3. His Imperial Majesty Emperor Haile Selassie I, originally named Tafari Makonnen, was born on 23 July 1892. He is a significant figure in both world history and Rastafarianism, and known for his leadership of Ethiopia. He ruled from 1930 until his overthrow in 1974, making him the last emperor of Ethiopia.
4. Rastafari, also known as Rastafarianism, is a spiritual and cultural movement that started in Jamaica during the 1930s. It promotes a way of life and belief system that emphasizes unity, spirituality and a connection to African heritage.
5. Van Gennep, A. (1960), *The Rites of Passage*. Translated by M. B. Vizedom and G. L. Caffee. Chicago: University of Chicago Press. (Original work published 1909).

NOTES

6. Turner, V. (1967), *The Forest of Symbols: Aspects of Ndembu Ritual*. Ithaca, NY: Cornell University Press.
7. The Slickers (1970s), *Johnny Too Bad*. On: *The Harder They Come* (Original Soundtrack). Island Records.
8. Henzell, P. (1972), *The Harder They Come* [Film]. Island Records.

BOOKIES

1. Pryce, K. (1979), *Endless Pressure: A Study of West Indian Lifestyles in Bristol*. Harmondsworth: Penguin Education.

EPILOGUE

1. This quote is often attributed to Stephen King from his work 'The Body', which was published in 1982.